THE BELL JAR

A Novel of the Fifties

TWAYNE'S MASTERWORK STUDIES

Robert Lecker, General Editor

THE BELL JAR

A Novel of the Fifties

LINDA WAGNER-MARTIN

TWAYNE PUBLISHERS • NEW YORK
Maxwell Macmillan Canada • Toronto
Maxwell Macmillan International • New York Oxford Singapore Sydney

Twayne's Masterwork Studies No. 98

The Bell Jar: A Novel of the Fifties
Linda Wagner-Martin

Twayne Publishers   Maxwell Macmillan Canada, Inc.
Macmillan Publishing Company   1200 Eglinton Avenue East
866 Third Avenue   Suite 200
New York, New York 10022   Don Mills, Ontario M3C 3N1

Macmillan Publishing Company is part of the Maxwell Communication Group of Companies.

Library of Congress Cataloging-in-Publication Data
Wagner-Martin, Linda.
    The bell jar, a novel of the fifties / Linda Wagner-Martin.
       p.   cm. — (Twayne's masterwork studies ; no. 98)
    Includes bibliographical references and index.
    ISBN 0-8057-8091-2 (alk. paper) — ISBN 0-8057-8561-2
(pbk. : alk. paper)
       1. Plath, Sylvia. Bell jar. I. Title. II. Series.
PS3566.L27B439   1992
813'.54—dc20   91-34025
                                                     CIP

10 9 8 7 6 5 4 3 2 1 (hc)
10 9 8 7 6 5 4 3 2 1 (pb)

Printed in the United States of America

For
Andrea Wagner

CONTENTS

NOTE ON THE REFERENCES AND ACKNOWLEDGMENTS

References to *The Bell Jar* throughout this text are from the Harper & Row edition of 1971.

I am indebted throughout this study to the work of Susan Van Dyne, Marjorie Perloff, and Melody Zajdel. Many thanks, too, to the several editors who have allowed me to reprint sections of essays previously published in their journals (*Women's Studies*, the *Journal of Narrative Technique*, the *Journal of American Culture*); to the Lilly Library Plath Archive at Indiana University and to the Smith Library Plath Archive at Smith College for permission to use various materials; and to Smith College and the Manuscripts Department, Lilly Library, Indiana University, Bloomington, Indiana, for permission to reprint the photo.

Sylvia Plath. Smith College yearbook

CHRONOLOGY:
SYLVIA PLATH'S LIFE AND WORKS

1932	Sylvia Plath born 27 October in Jamaica Plain, a part of Boston, Massachusetts, to Aurelia Schober and Otto Plath.
1936	The Plath family, including son Warren—born in the spring of 1935—moves to Johnson Avenue house in Winthrop Center, Massachusetts, near the Schober grandparents' home.
1938	Hurricane of 21 September (described in Plath's poems).
1940	Otto Plath dies of an embolism following surgery (complications from undiagnosed diabetes forced leg amputation). Sylvia and Warren do not attend funeral.
1942	The Plath family, now including the Schobers, moves to Wellesley, Massachusetts ("inland"), and Aurelia takes a teaching post at Boston University.
1942–1950	Sylvia attends public schools in Wellesley, excelling in academics and writing. Begins trying to publish work.
1950–1953	Scholarship student at Smith College as English major. Dates Dick Norton—family friend and Yalie—among others, 1951–53. Onset of first depression in spring.
1953	*Mademoiselle* College Board experience in New York during June. Returns to Wellesley for outpatient electroconvulsive shock treatments, administered for growing depression. Suicide attempt and recovery in sanatorium under care of skilled therapist Ruth Beuscher.
1954	Returns to Smith for spring semester. Begins planning honors thesis on Dostoyevski's use of the double.

1955 Graduates summa cum laude from Smith. Attends Newnham College, Cambridge, England, on Fulbright grant.

1956 Marries Ted Hughes, British poet, in England 16 June, with mother in attendance.

1957 Sylvia takes Cambridge degree. The couple moves to the United States while she teaches freshman English at Smith for a year.

1958 Ted and Sylvia move into Boston and live on their writing income. Sylvia also takes some part-time jobs, visits Robert Lowell's poetry class at Boston University, and becomes friends with Anne Sexton; resumes therapy with Ruth Beuscher.

1959 After a summer spent touring the United States in Aurelia Plath's car, Ted and Sylvia spend the fall at the writers' colony Yaddo. In December they sail for England; Sylvia never returns to the United States.

1960 Daughter Frieda Rebecca Hughes is born 1 April. Sylvia's first poem collection, *The Colossus*, is published in October.

1961 After living in London for more than a year, the Hugheses move to a fourteenth-century manor house in Devon. *The Bell Jar* drafted. Sylvia has a miscarriage and then undergoes an appendectomy.

1962 Nicholas Farrar Hughes is born 17 January. Sylvia writes *Three Women*, radio play for the BBC, and continues to work on the body of poetry that becomes the "Ariel" poems. Ted's infidelity causes separation and the angry incidents that appear in Sylvia's poems of the late summer and fall, particularly in October, when Ted moves from the Devon house. In December Sylvia and the children move to London, to "Yeats' house."

1963 Having composed the book she called *Ariel* in November 1962, Sylvia writes very different poems in 1963. Illness, the severe winter in England, and recurring depression lead to her suicide by asphyxiation 11 February. *The Bell Jar* appears in late January to good reviews, under the pseudonym Victoria Lucas.

1965 Ted publishes *Ariel*, and the cult of Plath begins.

1966 *The Bell Jar* is published in England under Plath's name.

1971 Ted publishes *Crossing the Water* and *Winter Trees*, additional collections from the late poems.

1981 *Sylvia Plath: The Collected Poems* is published; wins the Pulitzer Prize in poetry the following year.

1982 *The Journals of Sylvia Plath, 1950–1962* published only in the United States with Ted's admission in the Introduction that he had destroyed her last journal, and had lost the journal from early 1960 to her moving back to London.

Literary and Historical Context

1

America at Midcentury

The Bell Jar remains an accurate if frightening view of American life during the 1950s. There were few achieving women during that decade; the average age for women to marry had fallen to 20.3. As Douglas Miller and Marion Nowak conclude in *The Fifties: The Way We Really Were*, "Everybody got married in the fifties, or at least it was a supreme sign of personal health and well-being to be engaged in the social act of marriage and family-raising."[1] Accordingly, women were viewed as mates, and all kinds of "rights" came to be questioned—the value of education, for example, and the real intentions of childless couples. The nonmarried life-style was as suspect as deviant sexual behaviors (although those were not subjects one found in print during the 1950s), and pressure on women to marry—no matter how career oriented, how ambitious, how intelligent—was inescapable.

Plath's *Journals* are full of comments that show that pressure, and her anger about it. From Cambridge, England, as a Fulbright student, already a 23-year-old unmarried woman, she writes, "Suddenly everyone is very married and happy, and one is very alone, and bitter about eating a boiled tasteless egg by oneself every morning and painting on a red mouth to smile oh-so-sweetly at the world with." The duality of the 1950s plagues Plath; she does not want to marry and never have a career, but neither does she want to be some stereotype of the unfulfilled ("unwomanly") spinster. Where are her role models? "Why," she writes, "did Virginia Woolf commit suicide? Or Sara Teasdale. . . . Neurotic? Was their writing sublimation (oh horrible word). If only I knew. If only I knew how high I could set my goals, my requirements for my life."[2]

Plath's life was complicated even more by the fact that she was born into a highly educated family—but a family that tried, for various reasons, to copy the all-American structure. Otto Plath was a professor of entomology at Boston University, a German-born man who was 21 years his wife's senior when he married Aurelia Schober. She was then his student (in a class in German language), and she evidently continued to play that role throughout their marriage. As she admits in her candid introduction to Letters Home, "At the end of my first year of marriage, I realized that if I wanted a peaceful home—and I did—I would simply have to become more submissive, although it was not my nature to be so." Aurelia Plath's comments suggest that family life revolved around Otto and his projects. Their first year of marriage she dubs "the year of THE BOOK"; the second, "the year of THE CHAPTER." Not only did she write much of the material herself, but she arranged her household so that nothing would interfere with her husband's scholarship. If she wanted to use their dining-room table for something other than Otto's work, she would move all books and papers, after first making diagrams of their individual positions, and then carefully replace them.[3]

Such contrasting role models as the apparently submissive mother and the autocratic father played directly into the stereotypes rampant in the conservative 1950s women's magazines. When Plath read through the Ladies' Home Journals of her high school years—1946 through 1950—complete with the "undiscovered American beauty" on each cover, she saw almost nothing that would contradict her family pattern. Fiction, articles, poems, and particularly advertisements played incessantly on a single theme: the happy woman is the married woman. And younger readers were given articles with such titles as "Are You Worth Dating?" and "The Toughest Customer in the World Is the Man Who Doesn't Want to Marry." Woman's role—regardless of age—was to find, and keep, a boyfriend/husband. And the scaffolding of pursuit was the kind of sexual desire described in Farnham and Lundberg's *Modern Woman: The Lost Sex*. Thoroughly Freudian in its approach, this treatise showed that sexual satisfaction was gained through a woman's desire for motherhood. Doris Day's naive allure became the decade's model for sexiness, and women were allowed to be sensual and to enjoy sex so long as their sexual activity was devoted to one male partner. The assumption was that every person alive was heterosexual, and the birthrate rose incredibly during the 1950s. The national population grew 18.5 percent.[4]

It was a time of great material prosperity, corporate employment that focused on "family" involvement in sales quotas (so that wives were said to be a part of the company, and employees—almost exclusively male—were made conscious of the moral imperative to be loyal to both their families and their corporations), and many business-oriented moves. The nuclear, isolated family became the norm, a situation that meant women were handling every aspect of family life themselves, with no help from their families. Women with children had to become superwomen, as those children scurried to the various lessons and activities that marked the upwardly mobile family. At Smith, Sylvia Plath was introduced to the "suitable" occupations for women college graduates, and learned that charity work and volunteer activities—rather than paid employment—were to fill women's lives.

From Plath's perspective, as a college-age woman trying to find an appropriate direction for her life, these issues, as well as the anomie of the realities of the atom bomb, plagued her decision-making process. She voted for Adlai Stevenson (though her mother voted for Eisenhower) and lamented the McCarthyism, isolationism, and conservatism that had become pervasive American attitudes. *The Bell Jar* reflects her concern with women's choices, but its title speaks as well to the even more general stifling political atmosphere than the one that surrounds Esther Greenwood. The accomplishment of the novel is in part that its author was able to break through the bell jar of the confining 1950s patriarchal culture, to find her voice and her spirit as she identified herself as a writer. To have written both *The Bell Jar* and her later poems surely speaks of a kind of outright defiance of societal norms. One of the most important points to be made about Sylvia Plath and the 1950s is that she was *able* to become a writer. Without falling into the limiting roles that her culture tried to dictate for women of talent but slim financial means, she *became* a writer. *Take shorthand*, her mother admonished her. *Get married*, her friends urged. Do anything but go the way you are drawn—because writing is so insecure, so unsure, so masculine a profession. It is the ultimate risk. And what woman in the 1950s was being educated—intellectually or psychologically—to take risks? The contradiction between Plath's being a good daughter of a conservative middle-class home, highly conventional in its aims and moral systems, and trying to become a fine writer, living independently, traveling across Europe alone, living from day to day on writing income with no other security, seems unresolvable.

Once married to the British poet Ted Hughes, Plath somehow tried to subsume the aggressive writer figure she had willed herself to become into the docile yet sexy wife and homemaker (and, eventually, mother). That kind of change was one way of denying the real opposition inherent in what she had trained to become—a writer—and the role she was faced with becoming: a good wife, one who typed her husband's manuscripts and cooked with zeal and commitment. While it may be easier to relate Plath's suicide in 1963, at the age of 30, to the fact that her husband had taken a lover and that Plath was accordingly feeling the rejection every woman feels at betrayal, her death probably stemmed in part from the inherent contradiction between what American society thought her role was and what she insisted it must be. What Plath finally chose is not the primary topic of this study, but her death cannot be ignored. Women going into comparably complex and divided lives, making parallel choices, must realize that their occupational choices pose the inherent psychic risk of the ultimate divisiveness. *The Bell Jar* brings all that complexity before the reader again, giving it a veneer of comedy but insisting that Esther Greenwood's problems are more universal than individual.

2

The Importance of the Work

Some readers of *The Bell Jar* in the 1980s and the 1990s have been attracted to the novel because of Sylvia Plath's reputation as a cult writer. The beautiful and accomplished woman, dead by her own hand, has become a sort of martyr to women's rights, an implicit criticism of the midcentury social system that denied women ways to become professionals—that is, genuine people with lives of work and friendships outside primary sexual relationships.

The Bell Jar as novel, however, is meaningful and important as well for readers who know nothing about its author. It is a work that speaks for the disorientation of late adolescence, that confusing time when a person looks "adult" but is still dependent on parents, family, and teachers. While Esther Greenwood is female, the hesitancy and anxiety she feels are universal, and the novel's willingness to tell about those states of mind in a voice that has an undertone of comedy makes the narrative palatable to 1990s readers. In some respects, *The Bell Jar* has a great deal in common with Joseph Heller's *Catch-22* and J. D. Salinger's *The Catcher in the Rye*.

The fact that there were few literary novels about women characters made *The Bell Jar* seem "feminist" for its time, and the work was an attempt to write sympathetically about the problems inherent in growing up, particularly growing up female in the United States during the 1940s and the 1950s. Recognizing that women faced difficult decisions about their own and their family lives was in itself a feminist realization. Catharine Stimpson, writing 25 years after *The Bell Jar* was published, links the novel to Betty Friedan's *The Feminine Mystique*, "a vigorous polemic about a 'problem that had no name,' women's inferior position," as one of the causes of the revitalization of the twentieth-century feminist movement. As Ellen Moers had written in her 1976 *Literary Women*, "No writer has meant more to the current feminist movement."[5]

Charles Molesworth identifies another kind of importance for Plath's novel, that of the adolescent-as-social-misfit theme. Comparing *The Bell Jar* with *One Flew over the Cuckoo's Nest, An American Dream, Portnoy's Complaint, Herzog,* and *The Catcher in the Rye,* Molesworth links this tradition to Huck Finn as a means of imaging "the powerlessness of individuals in a mass, postindustrialist society." At variance with the dominant theme in earlier American literature— "the power of the single, sensitive personality"—this fiction that focuses on a protagonist doomed from the start often chooses the metaphor of illness or insanity as an ironic strategy.[6] Of the works mentioned, only *The Bell Jar* has a female protagonist.

Marilyn Yalom, writing in *Maternity, Mortality, and the Literature of Madness,* provides a crucial gloss for the use of the metaphor of madness by women writers, stating that a number of twentieth-century women writers have "appropriated literary insanity for their own ends and have endowed it with specifically female parameters. Many have emphasized the gender-related aspects of mental illness. . . . The best of these works possess a symbolic structure beyond the narrative line, with levels of meaning that elucidate the female situation in particular and the human condition in general. Thus, Sylvia Plath's story of her breakdown and recovery in *The Bell Jar* is simultaneously a pre-feminist exposé of the adverse effects of sexist culture on American women in the 1950s and . . . a pan-human myth of death and rebirth." Yalom's concern in explaining the wide relevance of Plath's novel is that in the context of women's madness, the role of motherhood has yet to be understood. It is her contention that society needs to question "the extent to which maternity, as option or experience, serves as catalyst for mental breakdown. A corollary of this question concerns the distinction between *maternity* and *motherhood*: to what extent is maternity (conception, pregnancy, parturition, lactation, and the nurturing of infants) a fixed biological, existentially loaded reality, and to what extent is motherhood (the daily care of children and the ensuing lifelong lien on the mother) a mutable social construct? How do maternity and motherhood in our society form a springboard toward madness?"[7] Yalom's critical perspective grew from the feminist and psychoanalytic criticism of the 1980s, yet Plath's own understanding of the depth of these issues was clearly in place more than 20 years earlier. *The Bell Jar* is a prescient work in that it anticipates later directions in critical theory.

Jerome Mazzaro places Plath's accomplishment in *The Bell Jar* in a less gendered category, seeing Esther's dilemma as illustrative of "Freud's formulaic allegorizing of human action into Ego and Id." While Mazzaro feels Plath's presentation of Freudian beliefs is negative, he thinks her novel is a classic statement of the midcentury fascination with, and acceptance of, Freudian prolegomena.[8]

The continued steady sales of Plath's novel—not only in the United States and England but throughout the world, translated into countless languages—show implicitly that her themes and characters are not dated, that the narrative *The Bell Jar* presents remains important for readers of the 1990s.

3

Critical Reception

Sylvia Plath's first book was a collection of poetry. Published in 1960 in England, *The Colossus* was well received, particularly in the United States. Plath was considered a respectable young poet whose work would bear watching. But when she chose to publish *The Bell Jar*—again in England and with the same publishers, the William Heinemann Company—in 1963, she used the pseudonym Victoria Lucas instead of her own name. Reviewers therefore had no idea that the author of this novel was an already-published poet, or that she was the (estranged) wife of a rising young British poet, Ted Hughes. *The Bell Jar*, then, when it appeared in mid-January 1963, was truly on its own.

Three of the novel's earliest reviews in January 1963 were consistently positive. Robert Taubman wrote in the *New Statesman* that this was a "clever first novel . . . the first feminine novel . . . in the Salinger mood." Critical comparison with J. D. Salinger's short stories and particularly his popular novel of adolescent breakdown, *The Catcher in the Rye*, occurred often, both in the British reviews of the the 1960s and in the American reviews of the early 1970s, when the novel finally appeared in a U.S. edition under Plath's real name. Writing in the

Listener, Laurence Lerner made no comparisons and seemingly had no reservations. He called the novel "a brilliant and moving book" that triumphed in "both language and characterization." Rupert Butler, too, found *The Bell Jar* "astonishingly skillful," "honest," "intensely interesting," "brave," and "terribly likeable."[9]

Later reviews were written about the novel as Plath's fiction, not that of Victoria Lucas, and were shadowed with the facts of both Plath's suicide on 11 February 1963 and the posthumous publication in 1965 of *Ariel*, the first collection of Plath's monumental late poems. Most reviewers saw parallels between *The Bell Jar* and the later poems, and many thought the fiction was inferior to the late poetry. In a 1966 editorial for *Critical Quarterly*, C. B. Cox praised *The Bell Jar* as an "extremely disturbing narrative" that made "compulsive reading." He then connected the novel with the poems: "The novel seems a first attempt to express mental states which eventually found a more appropriate form in the poetry. But throughout there is a notable honesty" and the same "fierce clarity so terrifying in the great poems in *Ariel*."[10]

M. L. Rosenthal, writing in the *Spectator*, also spoke of the novel's "magnificent sections whose candour and revealed suffering will haunt anyone's memory." He then continued in a vein that has become a touchstone for criticism about much of Plath's work: the cultural alienation—and resulting frustration—of the talented young woman. Rosenthal speaks of "the sense of having been judged and found wanting for no externally discernible reason, and the equally terrifying sense of great power gone to waste or turned against oneself."[11] In her 1972 *Hudson Review* essay, Patricia Meyer Spacks takes that tack as well when she calls the novel a good survey of the limited possibilities for women in midcentury America: "The sensibility expressed is not dismissable. The experience of the book is that of electrocution. . . . Female sexuality is the center of horror: babies in glass jars, women bleeding in childbirth, Esther herself thrown in the mud by a sadist, hemorrhaging after her single sexual experience. To be a woman is to bleed and burn. . . . Womanhood is entrapment, escaped from previously by artistic activity, escaped from surely only by death."[12] Lucy Rosenthal, writing in the *Saturday Review*, compares *The Bell Jar* to

Joan Didion's *Play It as It Lays* but points out that "the Plath mode is gentler." She praises the novel as "a deceptively modest, uncommonly fine piece of work . . . in its own right a considerable achievement. It is written to a small scale, but flawlessly—an artistically uncompromising, witty account."[13]

Juxtaposed with these comments should be Melvin Maddocks's caustic note that he finds the first half of the novel "Bobbsey Twins on Madison Avenue, gradually being disenchanted"; the second half, hardly related to the first, "less a contrast than a discontinuity." Martha Duffy, however, reviewing for *Time*, points out that the novel, eight years after its publication in England, is an American best-seller and refers to its "astonishing immediacy." Simultaneous with these American reviews in the early 1970s came Tony Tanner's opinion in his 1971 study, *City of Words: American Fiction, 1950–1970* that *The Bell Jar* was "perhaps the most compelling and controlled account of a mental breakdown to have appeared in American fiction." He called the work "a very distinguished American novel."[14]

Mason Harris, writing in 1973, stressed the connection with the "stifling hermetically-sealed world of the Eisenhower 'Fifties," praising the book because Plath's "distorted lens" of madness "gives an authentic vision of a period which exalted the most oppressive ideal of reason and stability. . . . If this novel goes less deeply into psychotic experience than Hannah Green's *I Never Promised You a Rose Garden* or Janet Frame's *Faces in the Water* it also does a much more complete job of relating the heroine's madness to her social world."[15] This is a key assessment for the 1980s and 1990s as well, when the novel both continues to speak for readers who feel trapped in the social paradigms that culture mandates and lends retrospective light to that period in midcentury America when Plath and her generation were trying to exist as achieving but still-subordinated women.

When *The Bell Jar* did appear in the United States, contrary to Mrs. Plath's apprehension that friends and relatives would be offended (and her resultant attempts to prohibit American publication of the novel), most reviews gave the work attention as a complex literary fiction. Although critics recognized that the phenomenal popularity of the book, and of Plath's *Ariel* poems, had created a cult of dedicated readers, assessments of the novel were well grounded and objective rather than sensationalized. When Helen Dûdar described the cult appreciation of *The Bell Jar*, she was careful to point out that the book's popularity rests on more than the deification of its author: filled with "wit and agony, the book represents recognizable experience."[16] With reviews by Ronald De Feo and Ruth Bauerle pointing to the fact that the novel is not simply autobiography,[17] some critics gave it serious attention. A Book-of-the-Month Club selection, the novel was also chosen as one of *Book World*'s "Fifty Notable Books" of 1971.

Currently, *The Bell Jar* is viewed as an integral part of Plath's oeuvre, its quality insisting that she thought of herself as much as a prose and fiction writer as a poet. Many readers believe the wry and quasi-comic mode of the novel provided Plath with the voice for many of the substantial late poems, the "light verse" (to use her irreverent phrase) of the *Ariel* collection: "Daddy," "Lady Lazarus," "The Detective," "The Applicant," and countless others. In her letters to friends about the novel, which she was planning to keep secret from her mother and other friends in America (precisely because she rightly predicted the hurt feelings that might occur over her fictionalizations of her college experiences), Plath described writing *The Bell Jar* as liberating. She enjoyed working "fiendishly" on it because it was such fun to see characters evolve and the wicked humor work.[18] As evidence of the real and unique power Plath had as a mature writer, *The Bell Jar* deserves the reading and recognition it continues to receive.

According to many critics of the 1980s, however, particularly those who employ feminist strategies, the efficacy of Plath's novel is caught in a time warp of midcentury thinking. Esther Greenwood's dilemma is real to the 1950s—but the times were changing. Had Plath not moved to England, by even the early 1960s she would have seen improvements in attitudes about women working and being independent. By the middle and later 1960s, the social revolt over racial and gender rights was in full bloom.

Many feminist readers are among those who find what Plath intended to be a positive ending marred by the biographical reality that Plath did kill herself. Although she may have left the institution pictured in *The Bell Jar* and grown healthy again, a decade later she was dead, a suicide. The implicit failure of the culture to be supportive, to find ways of helping Esther Greenwood/Sylvia Plath survive her times, conveys a relatively bleak message to contemporary readers.

Serious criticism has dealt with the problems of using Plath's novel as a classroom text, asking that teenage readers be given an approach that does not glamorize suicide. In the work of Susan Sniader Lanser and Teresa De Lauretis is prefigured the admonitory tendencies that become more noticeable as the 1980s continue: Plath's work, speaking as it does for a very restrictive period in contemporary American history, must be approached with some knowledge of history. Steven Axelrod's emphasis on *The Bell Jar* as a way for Plath to "reexperience her suffering and to retrieve her cure" is useful as a warning to readers who identify all too readily with Esther Greenwood's pain.[19]

Criticism by such critics as Lynda Bundtzen, Susan Bassnett, Paula Bennett, and Pamela Annas all points to the problem of the easy deification of Plath as a martyr. Jungian in focus, much of this work both underscores and ameliorates the sometimes-distracting identification between Plath and Greenwood, and allows the character in *The Bell Jar* to remain a fiction. Such an approach is, finally, healthful as well as health-giving.[20]

A Reading

4

The Bell Jar and Fictional Form

Even though millions of readers worldwide have been fascinated by Plath's novel, and sales have continued strong in the more than 20 years it has been available in the United States and translated into other languages, literary critics have trouble discussing *The Bell Jar*. Part of the difficulty is that the book defies simple literary categorization. Rather than being a single kind of novel, it is a blend of several structural types.

A fiction about a young person trying to make the central choices of late adolescence might well be a bildungsroman, a novel of education, with the outcome of the protagonist's choices being a successful adult life. In the canon of serious fiction, bildungsromans are usually about male protagonists, and the form reflects the kinds of lives men are free to choose—movement from small towns and villages to cities, involvement in a formal educational process, freedom to travel, separation from parents and family, involvement with a woman (or women) in the process of love affairs that provide both sexual experience to parallel educational experience and further avenues for exercising choice. The protagonist in this kind of novel makes both professional choices (what will I choose for a career? where will I live my life?) and personal ones (with whom will I live my life?).

Another kind of novel that would be appropriate for Plath's set of characters is the quest novel, a book in which the character sets off to find his or her idealistic and spiritual goal. The plot line of the fiction is frequently the journey itself, and often the journey is to find a religious symbol (i.e., the Holy Grail), some sign that the higher power, or God, has approved the journey and the person making it. Dating from the oldest known literature, the quest plot has either this religious aim or the philosophical one of finding truth (as in Oedipus's search to discover why his land is barren, what evil has befallen the country, only to find that his own personal actions of unknowingly killing his father and marrying his mother have brought down the curse). Narratively, the quest is the primary reason for the fiction, and it conveys a highly moral message through its outcome. In this tradition, brave, noble, and true protagonists are able to succeed, to find and conquer the objects of their searches.

Historically, both the bildungsroman and the quest novel usually had male protagonists. Each involved travel, living apart from society and family, experiencing physical danger—and for much existing literary history, women characters could not have undertaken such lives. As soon as a woman character left the protection of her family to live alone, by her own wits, society saw her as "fallen" and the moral intention of the plot was destroyed. The best statement of the difficulty of writing these conventionally structured fictions about women characters is Virginia Woolf's discussion of Judith Shakespeare, a fictional persona Woolf creates in her 1928 essay, *A Room of One's Own*, to illustrate how impossible living a male life would have been for women.

Woolf points out the difficulty of leaving home, finding a place in the city, and securing work as she creates the talented Judith Shakespeare (William Shakespeare's "sister"). Even if Judith had exactly the same talents and ambition as her brother, she would not have been educated, she would not have been able to live as an actor, and no one would have taken her writing for the stage seriously. In fact, in Woolf's words Judith does run away from home and the arranged marriage that faced her there: "The force of her own gift alone drove her to it. . . . She had the quickest fancy, a gift like her brother's, for the tune of words. Like him, she had a taste for the theater. She stood at the stage door; she wanted to act, she said. Men laughed in her face." After being ridiculed and rebuffed, this 16-year-old was taken in hand by "Nick Greene the actor-manager." Later, "she found herself with child by that gentleman and so—who shall measure the heat and violence of the poet's heart when caught and tangled in a woman's body?—killed herself one winter's night and lies buried at some cross-roads where the omnibuses now stop outside the Elephant and Castle!"[21]

Woolf's fictional Judith Shakespeare haunts the mind of every woman who has ever wanted to be a writer, who has ever wanted to succeed in what society sees as "a man's world," and even though she is a fictional construct, her story runs parallel to that of Esther Greenwood in *The Bell Jar*, for Esther has personal ambitions. She sees herself as something other than a wife, or other than primarily a wife, though she does not want to give up the female experience of loving a mate, having children, and leading a satisfying domestic life.

Esther's personal choices are much like Plath's narrative choices in that some patterns seem to be restricted to male characters. The novel that would allow a woman character to be its protagonist, its hero, is the domestic or marriage novel. As the name suggests, this type of fiction takes place within a stable social world, often within the house (the reason it is called "domestic"), and gains its narrative interest from a romantic-love plot. The form of this novel mirrors the culture that suggests women have only one role in life—to marry—and therefore the chief "plot" of women's lives is choosing a suitable husband. The domestic novel also usually places the woman into her family household as daughter; her marriage then becomes the means of the family members controlling her life, and perhaps increasing their fortune, if the match is a good one. The woman character is drawn, first, as the daughter of the home, the child of the patriarchy, under the control of the father. As she matures, she becomes the wife of another male character, so that control of her has passed from one man to another. While the other women characters in this kind of novel sympathize with the protagonist and try to support her, they have so little power themselves that they cannot really effect much change. The protagonist is at the mercy of the control the patriarchy wants to exercise.

What seems most important about the domestic novel is that the marriage is seen as the means for the patriarch of the family—the father—to ensure his daughter's safekeeping and security by handing her over to the man he has chosen to husband her. The female character is therefore dependent throughout: if not in her father's care, she is under the wing of her husband.

While *The Bell Jar* has certain elements of this fictional pattern, it is also clear that the pattern is one of the objects of Plath's satire. *The Bell Jar* in some ways parodies the domestic novel because so much of Esther's energy is spent trying to avoid marrying the "suitable" suitor her family has in effect chosen for her. The role of Buddy Willard becomes much more important than it might seem in the plot itself because his character represents the most "reasonable" choice Esther has before her.

The more sensationalized romance novel is a defiant stepchild of the marriage novel, because in a romance novel the woman character usually decides to choose a mate for herself and often he is not a man acceptable to her family. Whether motivated by passion or anger, the woman character chooses a mate that defies her father's choice, in some kind of attempt to end family control and achieve her own independence of choice. Both kinds of novels work from the paradigm that the successful woman character becomes the married woman; indeed, to be "successful" is to be successful in love. If the woman character is truly successful, she marries the man of her choice (regardless of what her family thinks). If she is less successful, she marries not the man of her choice but some other man. (But at least she marries—that is the "happy ending" for this narrative form.) If, however, she is an obvious failure socially and romantically, she does not marry and instead becomes the old maid, the visiting aunt, the unwanted, the woman who loved and lost, and so on. Western literature is filled with such unsuccessful women characters, many placed in such untenable positions within the narrative that they choose death, often suicide, as a reasonable alternative to the stigma of being unmarried. The power of Buddy Willard's last wounding comment to Esther, "I wonder who you'll marry now, Esther" (and then repeated, for emphasis and for instructing Esther, who seems not to understand the full import of his question), "I wonder who you'll marry now, Esther. Now you've been . . . here"[22] stems partly from the social fabric that defines woman's role as partner in marriage. The chances of Esther's marrying well, after her recent, well-publicized history of psychic breakdown and care, have diminished considerably. She is no longer a "normal" Smith College student; she is a woman with a frightening past. Even if Esther has long since denied the cultural power of having to be married, she must still live successfully within the culture that enforces this belief, and doing so will be as difficult as leaving the hospital at the end of the novel.

Plath's *The Bell Jar*, then, has elements of each of these forms,[23] and several of the following sections will discuss in detail the ways the author both uses and avoids parts of these narrative conventions. But *The Bell Jar* also has a narrative voice, that of Esther Greenwood remembering, telling most of her story from the vantage point of health and security (she is evidently married and a mother), casting the events as if they were some fragments of a long-past bad dream. The difficulty Esther's voice creates for the reader, at least in some parts of the novel, is that it is written to be intentionally comic. Comedy in a novel about a woman's suicide attempt, breakdown, and hospitalization—among other relatively unpleasant plot lines—seems inappropriate if not macabre.

The pseudocomedy of the narrator's voice works with Plath's highly fragmented narrative structure, in which events are glimpsed briefly in one place only to reappear in more detail later, to create a structure that intentionally keeps the reader off-balance. Just as its genre is not easily defined, so are the voice and tone of *The Bell Jar* enigmatic, if not actually confusing. Plath's almost-overwhelming number of images and metaphors also work to change what seems to be the obvious narrative direction (what effect do the arrow images, the fig tree metaphor, the drowning and graveyard images have on the narrative?). Although *The Bell Jar* is comparatively short, it is a complex mixture of various tones of voice, events, images, and narratives. Readers who come to the work with certain kinds of limited literary expectations are sometimes less successful in their reading than readers willing to trust Plath's own directions are.

The Bell Jar does indeed provide its own map for good reading, and in the author's successful structural control—as the novel moves episode by episode, line by line, word by word—the reader can find the clues necessary to unraveling this complex fiction. Tonally, for example, the title—the stark image of "bell jar"—could be either quasi-scientific or ominous. To be placed within a bell jar, a glass-enclosed, confined space for the purpose of being observed, caught in a vacuum, separated from the rest of life, would probably be a negative experience. To be such an observed object, and be female, suggests one of the image patterns important to the later feminist movement—that all too often women are seen as objects, as possessions, of their men and their culture. Therefore, Plath's use of the idea of being located as a scientific object, staked out as it were for the explicit purpose of observation, can be only negative and dehumanizing.

The title phrase itself includes the word *bell*, which when spelled differently, as *belle*, was meant in the nineteenth century to be a positive term in American culture—the "belle" of the ball, the ladylike southern woman with many suitors, a "belle," and, by implication, a woman who knew her role and was happy to be the desired object of her lover and family. The tension between (a) the reader's immediate reading of *bell*, evoking the more nostalgic and sexualized *belle*, and (b) the clipped monosyllable that follows it—*jar*—is part of what gives the reader the uneasy feeling that this fiction is not quite what it seems. As a verb, *jar* is by definition unsettling, keeping one off-balance. As a noun, it names either the enclosure necessary for scientific observation or the domestic container the housewife uses to can fruits or vegetables. The difference between *jar* and another synonym, *glass*, suggests that Plath wanted the abruptness and imbalance of the word she chose.

The author's opening paragraph—and the choices she as the controller of narrative makes in writing it—continues to unsettle the reader: "It was a queer, sultry summer, the summer they electrocuted the Rosenbergs, and I didn't know what I was doing in New York. I'm stupid about executions. The idea of being electrocuted makes me sick, and that's all there was to read about in the papers—goggle-eyed headlines staring up at me on every street corner and at the fusty, peanut-smelling mouth of every subway. It had nothing to do with me, but I couldn't help wondering what it would be like, being burned alive all along your nerves." And in a separate paragraph all to itself, this sentence: "I thought it must be the worst thing in the world" (1).

The tone of the opening paragraph is reinforced through this single-line paragraph that leaves the reader no choice but to understand how emphatic the as-yet-unnamed protagonist is about death. Her word choice in this opening, however, is much more vivid than the word *death* would be. Her phrasing is "executions," "electrocuted" (used twice), and "being burned alive all along your nerves." The intensity of this naming process—even though the narrative voice tries to distance herself, saying, "It had nothing to do with me"—reveals the character's horror at people's being killed because they have broken a cultural rule. Allegedly, the Rosenbergs were giving Russia political information. Allegedly, they were spies. The case, however, was never proved conclusively, and the media made much of the fact that Julius and Ethel Rosenberg were husband and wife, and were also the parents of two young children.

This seemingly oblique opening is carefully structured and chosen. The beginning of any novel featuring a young woman protagonist has a great deal to do with the reader's expectations about the kind of novel such a protagonist would be appropriate to. If this is a domestic novel, then the young married couple—the Rosenbergs—have met an unexpected end, despite their success as married people and as parents. The viciousness of their deaths—electrocution as Plath describes it, "being burned alive"—calls into question the social code that creates such torture. (It was not many years until capital punishment itself was made illegal in a number of states.) And in archetypal terms, the fact that the narrative begins during the summer coinciding with the

Rosenbergs' execution is also a reversal of the reader's expectations. Rather than the flowering, the full bloom of summer, this summer brings a withering and a death. The "heat" Esther endures is more akin to the terrible burning of the electrocution than it is to a natural summer climate.

If *The Bell Jar* were to be read as a quest novel, the location of the action would be critical. Plath seems to emphasize that the narrative is occurring in New York, a city Esther does not know and heretofore has never visited. Yet Esther's behavior is not typical of someone learning a location: she reads newspapers rather than maps; she is confronted with the opening to a transportation system described as a "stale mouth," not some exotic route to full understanding or adventure. Both the location of the city and the character's means to travel within it are described negatively, as if to suggest that the protagonist's traditional activities are doomed from the start.

The voice of the protagonist is itself problematic. In the midst of a strange city, surrounded by happenings upsetting to herself, her friends, and the almost-mythical Rosenbergs, Esther Greenwood refuses either to be serious or to take seriously herself (and her dilemma of lostness). The voice that instructs the reader is off-putting; it is defeated and defeating. "I didn't know what I was doing in New York," Esther says. How much confidence can the reader have in this narrator, if she doesn't even know the simplest kind of traditional narrative information? "I'm stupid about executions" is another purposely antagonistic statement. Protagonists, even young ones, are the center of the reader's interest; why would the reader be interested in a character who announces her stupidity? Readers of most novels would hope to be given a protagonist who can succeed, not someone slated for failure from the start. Why doesn't the character know what she is doing in New York? Why does she consider herself stupid? Bothered by these questions, the reader is not sure he or she believes the narrator when she says, in the single-paragraph sentence, "I thought it must be the worst thing in the world." Plath's emphatic summary sentence has as little closure as the rest of the opening, and leaves the text open to the reader's question, Why does the character only "think" such a death is terrible? Any death is probably "the worst thing in the world"; what makes death by electrocution so appalling to the narrator?

Plath's strategy in her opening plays on the reader's familiarity with twentieth-century first-person narrative conventions. In a usual first-person narrative, the reader has some acceptance of the narrative voice. The first-person technique allows the reader to feel close to the character, to understand the character's motivations, because the process of language allows greater insight into the workings of the character's mind, moral values system, and personality. In *The Bell Jar*, however, Plath is intentionally interfering with the confidence the reader expects to have in the narrative voice. She is making the reader question the credibility of that voice.

Why Plath does this in *The Bell Jar* becomes clear after the first few paragraphs. "I knew something was wrong with me that summer," Esther finally says. Our narrator is, then, by the author's own admission, behaving atypically. She is ill, mentally upset, depressed, lost in this unusual experience of being in New York on a scholarship, and yet obsessed (by her own admission) with the Rosenberg execution. Plath's narrative voice is constructed to be abnormal, unreliable, yet her choosing of this voice also conveys important information to the reader. Esther Greenwood may be unstable now, she may be questioning every opinion, every motivation, every thought—but she is still healthy enough to know she is going through an unusual experience. What makes her illness in the hot New York summer the epitome of fear and frustration is that no one connected with her recognizes she is ill. Her world of friends and family understands her so little or—she fears—cares so little about her that she can fool everyone about her mental and physical state. To be so successful at disguising her very real health problems is the tragedy of Esther's experience.

Even though Plath makes no secret of the problems of her protagonist, one difficulty in sorting through the narrative lines in the novel is the speed at which the impressions are conveyed, as well as the range of different metaphors the narrator chooses. It is literally hard at times to figure out what is being said. Because the narrator jumps quickly between objective statements and her own reaction to them, the reader is asked to fuse two kinds of information—factual information, about the external events of this period, and subjective information, about the protagonist's state of mind, which the reader must infer from assessing the protagonist's reactions to those external events. The information is made even more difficult to access because it is so concentrated, telescoped into a single paragraph, when full exploration of either the Rosenberg situation or Esther's reaction to the death penalty could easily take pages of text.

The prose style in itself is meant to convey the mental anguish of the protagonist, so disoriented that she grasps at pieces of information, races to another topic, returns to the first, and then breaks any rational progression into fragments by inserting her own highly personal, informal, and sometimes-intentionally comic reactions between the sentences that express her thoughts. The jerky movement from inner to outer states of mind serves to disconcert the reader, and the first section of the novel (of only nine short paragraphs, fewer than two pages of text) leaves the reader breathless. Most novels do not have such an effect. The speed and fragmentation of Esther's narrative provides the best clue for the kind of interior monologue Plath is creating.

By the early 1960s, American and British readers had been thoroughly trained in reading stream-of-consciousness, first-person fiction. William Faulkner's 1929 *The Sound and the Fury*, with its monologue of Benjy Compson, a retarded child, occupying the first quarter of the novel, and James Joyce's 1922 *Ulysses*, with its several interior monologues, had established the pattern for the voiced narrative that expressed the highly subjective interior life of the character. Sylvia Plath, an outstanding English major at Smith College and at Newnham College in England, had studied these works, as well as others that used the modernist narrative technique, and knew she was working in a highly visible, frequently taught narrative tradition. Yet few critics at the time described the opening monologue of *The Bell Jar* in narratively sophisticated terms. They seemed to read instead a young woman protagonist who was a conventional product of her times, the American fifties—scatterbrained, flighty, and "stupid," to draw on Plath's own ironic vocabulary. These critics seemed to assume that young American women of college age in the fifties were like Esther Greenwood. Such acceptance of the character as "normal," representative of her times, completely devalued what Plath was trying to present: a woman caught in a state of instability that remained undetectable to the outer world. In one sense, Plath's work was caught in the problem of gendered responses to literature: male readers expected certain things from women novelists, and from women characters. For Plath to expect such readers to read the seriously disturbed Esther as atypical, when their culture devalued any woman who was accomplished, was going against the grain of fictional practice at midcentury.

Once the reader comprehends that Esther Greenwood's voice is not meant to be her normal voice, then following the narrative of *The Bell Jar* becomes a poignant and sad experience. The supposed comedy the novel achieves is never pure comedy; it is always tempered with the reader's sympathy for Esther. The drama Plath creates is the reader's urgent involvement with the character of Esther Greenwood—wanting her to find help, wanting the people around her to understand the disruption that has occurred in her life and to help her rather than ignore all the danger signals she shows so clearly.

5

The Bell Jar as Layered Narrative

The effect of *The Bell Jar* is layered as the reader comes to understand the difficulties of Esther's expressing what she feels, in the context of her own depression and disillusion. The reader, then, is faced with the same circumstances Esther faces: having to find a way to voice her narrative and yet live within a family and a culture that responds to her problems in useless ways, if at all.

Plath's division of the novel into 20 chapters is another means of making the reader empathize with the protagonist's frustration. These chapters are themselves divided into segments, so that many narrative units constitute any single story. Chapter 1, for example, has three separate parts. The first segment concerns Esther's disillusionment over the Rosenberg situation and ends with several images of the narrator's being out of control and powerless within her culture (the metaphor of Esther's "steering" New York like a car, supposedly being in the driver's seat; the metaphor of promise evaporating "like the tail end of a sweet dream" and that lost dream's later connection with the myth of the American dream; the metaphor of the floating head of the cadaver, following Esther like a balloon and melding with the face of her boyfriend, Buddy Willard).

The Bell Jar as Layered Narrative

The second segment is a description of the prizewinning college women running the *Mademoiselle* College Board during early summer, living together in the Amazon Hotel in New York. This segment focuses on (a) Doreen, the group's defiant and irrepressible beauty, whose sexuality speaks for Esther's more repressed sensual self, and (b) Doreen's opposite, Betsy, the western innocent who is loved by her elders and friends but whose sunny demeanor has drawn from Doreen the name "Pollyanna Cowgirl."

The third segment is a culmination of the first two parts. Here Plath sets up a narrative duel between the "evil" (sensual) Doreen and the "good" Betsy, through Esther's leaving the taxi convoy that is taking the dozen women to a formal dance, and going with Doreen to a bar, escorted by the disreputable disc jockey Lenny Shepherd, who drinks, sets up sexual plots, and involves Doreen in sexual behaviors that frighten Esther. Lenny as a devil figure rather than a shepherd heightens the polarity of Esther's choices between Doreen and Betsy, choices that are really more central to her own development in that they are choices she will make about her own behavior and manner.

Chapter 1, for all its quick movement from scene to scene and image to image, serves to introduce several of Plath's central narrative lines. One important theme is that a woman character cannot be seen as "individual"; she is always a part of her culture. Unlike a Thoreau, who can go to live as he pleases beside a secluded pond, Esther Greenwood—whose name suggests she shares Thoreau's bond with nature—is subjected to deciding what role within society she will play. Her choice is not to leave that society; escape is not an option. And the woman character in her culture faces continuous decisions. Will Esther sympathize with the Rosenbergs? As human beings, they are being killed in a terrible way. They are being violated not only by being killed but by "being burned along their nerves." Yet they have broken rules; they have been traitors to their country. Implicit in the consideration of the Rosenberg matter is Esther's dilemma—can she break social rules? Can she live the kind of life she wants, regardless of what her culture says? The Rosenbergs are being punished for their disobedience, or perhaps for their difference. What, then, will happen to Esther, who feels herself very different from most of her peers? In the patriarchal hierarchy, duty to one's culture, one's country, is paramount. In the matriarchal hierarchy, duty to one's psychological or emotional self may be more important, or so Plath's juxtaposition of parts 1 and 2 within chapter 1 suggests. For Esther, the dilemma she faces in living with the other College Board editors is deciding which woman to befriend. One represents the kind of sexual freedom that Esther's social group, her class, and her mother would find reprehensible; the other is the same kind of woman Esther is and always has been.

Along with making this choice of friends comes a sexual agenda: to live as Betsy does is to remain safe. To live as Doreen does is to invite sexual experience. What will be the result of sexual intercourse? In the domestic novel, the woman character's commodification and her success in the marriage market depend on her being a virgin. Esther is all too aware of how crucial her virginity is to her social and moral well-being (not to mention her eventual economic well-being). Yet the greatest temptation of her New York experience is that she become sexually experienced. *The Bell Jar* shows that sexual maturity carries risks only for women: the Buddy Willard affair shows him unscathed publicly. For women, however, sexual experience can change lives. Even if one does not become pregnant, one loses value in the marriage market. Perhaps worse, one may become sexually enthralled to some partner who is not appropriate as a future husband.

Chapter 1 of *The Bell Jar* is truly introductory, then, even though its three segments differ appreciably from one another. The themes of Esther's story are themselves multiple, as well as complex, and cannot be presented in any simple linear fashion. Choices come to Esther in a whirl of action; separating the strands of those choices is difficult, particularly in this atypical time of confusion for her. Such a structural format occurs in many of the other chapters, as Plath uses the physical break in print—the blank white space—to signal a change in narrative time, sometimes a flashback, sometimes a flash-forward, sometimes a different narrative section. Other of the chapters are single-focused, telling the same story throughout. Elementary as the technique of fragmentation is, Plath uses it effectively and usually helps the reader sort through the several strands of plot that compose the book.

Esther Greenwood's story, as the narrative structure shows, is a montage of past experiences and present happenings. More accurately, it is a montage of past experiences seen through the lens of present happenings, with the reader being continually apprised of the significance of those past happenings. Signaling the reader from chapter 1, when the image of the cadaver associated with Buddy Willard appears as a balloon over Esther's shoulder, omnipresent in her mind, Plath forces a number of scenes, objects, and reflections into the fragmented but relentless stream that makes up Esther's consciousness. Even though the story is hers, Plath's method makes it seem external rather than subjective: events exist as events, even though they are told in Esther's voice. Plath creates a narrative method that draws from the devices of stream of consciousness but is less overwhelmed by the personal than most narratives of this kind. This distancing allows the sense of comedy, of ridicule and parody, at no loss of the reader's sympathy for Esther.

Plath's mixture of tones and narratives, achieved partly through her inventive point of view and her juxtaposed and fragmented sections of story, is one of the most effective devices in *The Bell Jar*. Reading pace varies surprisingly. A slow dramatic section is contrasted with a fast-moving comic recollection, just as one chapter that is composed of several plot segments is set between chapters that are single narratives. In this impressionistic collage structure, Plath has a great deal of freedom to choose which episodes to tell, and perhaps retell, and at which times: there is no chronologically ordered external framework. The initial reference to Buddy Willard's taking Esther on a day's visit to his university hospital—viewing the live birth, the fetuses in jars, the cadaver—occurs in the first segment of chapter 1. The recounting of that day in detail, however, is left until chapter 6, when the events become a crucial part of Esther's description of Buddy's grasp for control of their relationship. After the frightening descriptions of the cadaver, the macabre fetuses, classes in diseases, and the baby's birth—during which time Esther's sheer factual ignorance depresses her

("Why was it all covered with flour?" [54] she asked after the child is born), Buddy takes her to his room, where they drink wine and Esther reads poetry to him. The reader is made aware—as is Esther—that Esther's knowledge is no match for Buddy's, and through his dividing knowledge so that everything scientific belongs in his province, he has effectively assumed control of their relationship.

Plath makes this clear by choosing to include medical situations pertaining to women's health and reproductive processes: each of the medical segments has to do with women and women's lives. A beautiful young woman with a black mole dies in 20 days. Fetuses are put in jars and observed, the products of some female body—and the evidence of the forbidden sexual experience that haunts Esther throughout the book. Mrs. Tomolillo's birthing the baby serves to show the woman-as-mother treated mechanically, drugged so that she knows nothing, drugged to erase the memory of the terrible pain that is so evident to everyone watching the delivery. Worse, the delivery itself is in incompetent hands, as the young medical student, Buddy's friend Will, panics and keeps repeating, " 'I'm going to drop it, I'm going to drop it, I'm going to drop it,' in a terrified voice" (54).

That the delivery itself should be the object of students' spectatorship diminishes Esther's sense of the woman's primary role in the birth and prefigures a 1980s attention on the power—the destructive power—of the "male gaze." Mrs. Tomolillo is only an object, an insensate and unconscious object, hardly a positive model for Esther as she thinks of her own life role, to marry and give birth to children.

The structural ending of this scene, with Buddy attempting to continue his "instruction" of Esther by showing her his penis and presumably arousing her sexually, undercuts the tragedy of Esther's realization, for as Buddy undresses, Plath turns the would-be sensual scene into broad comedy. Buddy's "underpants" are laughable: " 'They're cool,' he explained, 'and my mother says they wash easily' " (55). Buddy's remark is hardly appropriate to this seduction scene, and the implication that he is still his mother's little boy, wearing clothes that she chooses and doing what she instructs, is indelibly planted. Once Mrs. Willard becomes a part of the scene, it is easy for

Esther to remain distanced from the emotion of the encounter: "Then he just stood there in front of me and I kept staring at him. The only thing I could think of was turkey neck and turkey gizzards and I felt very depressed" (55).

A simple scene that deflates decades of Freudian critique about "penis envy" among women, this comic statement by Esther sets the tone for the further action, as Buddy urges, in a mockery of adult language, "Now let me see you" (56). By placing Buddy's speech at the level of preschoolers, Plath subverts the would-be eroticism and destroys the power Buddy has been trying to accumulate.

Later ramifications of the scene, as well as the visit to the medical school, include Esther's discovery that Buddy—contrary to his facade and his family's social code—is no longer a virgin. His sexual experience throughout the summer with an older waitress at his camp has made his interest in Esther seem the greatest hypocrisy—his being thrilled at the effects of her supposedly experienced kisses, his devotion to her as a woman of wide sexual knowledge. Plath turns this narrative development into comedy as well, by bringing Buddy's mother back into the conversation. Esther asks, "What does your mother think about this waitress?" (57), and that entry allows Esther to comment on Buddy's closeness to his mother, her scrutiny of his friend's morals, and her real role in the novel, which is as spokesperson for the dominant 1950s gender ideology: "What a man wants is a mate and what a woman wants is infinite security," and "What a man is is an arrow into the future and what a woman is is the place the arrow shoots off from" (58). Locating these offensive homilies with Mrs. Willard (who is always referred to in this wifely role, never by her first name) allows Plath to include women in her criticism of gender politics in the 1950s, a time when women, too, accepted the stereotyped roles society urged them into. Mrs. Willard exhausts herself getting up before dawn to pack huge, and money-saving, picnic lunches for trips. She uses her free time to weave equally money-saving rugs for household floors. And in between times, she mouths the restricting maxims that pepper *The Bell Jar*, blocks in the verbal wall that keep Esther feeling so separate from her culture that she finally tries to commit suicide.

The chapter ends, however, not with the comic "seduction" scene but with a phone call from Buddy (who never calls, because of the expense). Distraught and shaken from the news that he has contracted tuberculosis and will have to go to a sanatorium for a year, Buddy begs Esther to write to him, to visit him over Christmas, to remain his girlfriend. Esther immediately feels a delicious freedom—though she pretends their relationship is serious, so that she can have some peace in her house and get some work done.

The gendered text is emphasized, however, as Plath employs the scene to reinscribe the ways the male medical student has used his knowledge to control Esther: "I had never heard Buddy so upset. He was very proud of his perfect health and was always telling me it was psychosomatic when my sinuses blocked up and I couldn't breathe. I thought this an odd attitude for a doctor to have and perhaps he should study to be a psychiatrist instead, but of course I never came right out and said so" (59). Esther speculates that the tuberculosis might be a punishment for Buddy's living his false, double-standard sexual life; still, what she primarily feels is relief. She can legitimately be a college woman with a boyfriend ("practically engaged") and stay in on weekend nights to study. It is the best of both worlds in a world that, as *The Bell Jar* shows, is not arranged to allow women freedom, choice, or happiness.

6

The Bell Jar as Bildungsroman

No matter how Plath arranges her narrative, the primary plot concerns Esther Greenwood living her life as a college woman—having adventures outside the family home and protection; being faced with choices about career, sexual activities, and moral values; and asking herself questions about the people she chooses for friends, as well as about her professional and erotic choices. In this concentration, Plath's novel is a bildungsroman. According to Jerome Buckley in his study of this form, its principal elements are "a growing up and gradual self-discovery," "alienation," "the conflict of generations," "ordeal by love," and "the search for a vocation and a working philosophy."[24]

By setting the novel first in New York, Plath can separate Esther not only from her family but from all the college friends who would notice abnormal behavior. In New York, Esther is both isolated and alienated. Moreover, the New York scenario is made to serve an important purpose for the true story of Esther's development. The seemingly innocent, even boring episodes about the college women's doing assignments, going to lunches and dances, buying clothes, dating men, and sorting through life-styles that shock, bewilder, and yet fascinate are given unexpected drama because they are plotted to establish Plath's two central themes: (a) that of Esther's developing identity, or lack thereof, and (b) that of her battle against submission to the authority of both older people and, more visibly, men. Although the second theme is sometimes absorbed by the first, Plath uses enough imagery of sexual conquest that each comes to have equal importance. For a woman of the 1950s, finding an identity other than that of sweetheart, girlfriend, and wife and mother was a major achievement.

Esther's search for identity is described first through a series of episodes involving the possible role models of Doreen and Betsy. Throughout these events, Plath focuses the reader's attention on Esther's diminishing sense of self: Esther describes herself as a photo negative, as a small black dot, as a hole in the ground. When she returns to her hotel after her 48-block walk, she does not recognize herself in the mirror—some Chinese woman, she thinks, "wrinkled and used up." Later, she sees herself as "the reflection in a ball of dentist's mercury" (20–21). Purging in a hot bath, Esther temporarily escapes her own consciousness and that of everyone else: "Doreen is dissolving, Lenny Shepherd is dissolving, Frankie is dissolving, New York is dissolving, they are all dissolving away and none of them matter any more. I don't know them, I have never known them and I am very pure" (22).

The second story Plath chooses to tell of the New York experience concerns the ptomaine poisoning of all the women except Doreen after the *Ladies' Day* luncheon. Because the vignette of Jay Cee's disappointment with Esther's lack of ambition is embedded in this scene, Esther takes the opportunity of recuperating from her near death to assess the female role models before her: her own mother, who urges her to learn shorthand so that she will be able to find a job; the successful writer Philomena Guinea, who has befriended her but done so prescriptively; and the editor Jay Cee, by now an admonitory figure. Although after her poisoning, Esther feels "purged and holy and ready for a new life" (52), she cannot rid herself of the feeling of having been betrayed, for no sooner has she decided Jay Cee would be her mentor ("I wished I had a mother like Jay Cee. Then I'd know what to do") than Jay Cee has disappointed her. Plath's handling of these episodes makes clear

Esther's confusion about her direction. As Buckley points out, the apparent conflict with parent or place in the traditional bildungsroman is secondary to the real conflict, which remains "personal in origin; the problem lies with the hero himself [or herself]" (Buckley, 20).

Esther's struggle to know herself, to be self-directed and motivated, is effectively presented through the fragmented narrative structure. As Patricia Spacks has written about the literature of the adolescent, the adolescent character has no self to discover. The process is not one of discovering a persona already there but rather one of creating that persona.[25] Unlike Esther, then, the reader should perhaps not be disturbed that the face in her mirror is mutable. We must recognize with sympathy, however, that Esther carries the weight of having to maintain a number of often-conflicting identities—the obliging daughter and the ungrateful woman, the successful writer and the immature student, the virginal girlfriend and the worldly lover. Through its structure, the novel shows how closely these strands are interwoven.

The presence of Buddy Willard—although he is not in New York as a participant in any of these episodes—underscores what a blank page Esther is. Whatever this college woman is during the summer of 1953, she has developed in that direction because of the indoctrination of her socially approved guide, Buddy Willard. For Buddy, women are helpmeets; they are to have no identity in themselves. Esther's poems are "dust," and her role is to be virginal and accepting of his direction—whether the terrain be sex or skiing. More explicit than their conversations are the images Plath chooses to describe Esther during this section, images of frustration and futility.

One central image is the fig tree, first introduced after Esther has nearly died from the food poisoning and is reading stories the magazine has sent to the convalescents. Lush in its green spring, the fig tree nourishes young love. In contrast, Esther describes her love for Buddy as a kind of dying: "we had met together under our own imaginary fig tree, and what we had seen wasn't a bird coming out of an egg but a baby coming out of a woman, and then something awful happened and we went our separate ways" (61). When the fig tree image recurs to Esther, she sees it filled with fat purple (phallic, perhaps) figs: "one fig was a husband and a happy home and children, and another fig was a famous poet and another fig was a brilliant professor, and another fig was Ee Gee, the amazing editor" (84–85). She sits frustrated in the crotch of the tree, however, "starving to death, just because I couldn't make up my mind which of the figs I would choose. I wanted each and every one of them, but choosing one meant losing all the rest." The dilemma of Esther's adolescence—unlike that of most men—was that any choice was also a relinquishing. Esther believed firmly that there was no way, in the American society of the 1950s, that a talented woman could successfully combine a career with homemaking.

Eventually, in Esther's metaphor, the figs rot and die, a conclusion that aligns the image tonally with the rest of the novel's metaphors. In her highly visual presentation of Esther's education, Plath consistently shows characters who are poisoned, diseased, injured, bloodied, and even killed. The violence of this pattern of characterization parallels the intensity of Esther's feelings as she matures. (Again, in Spacks's words, "The great power implicitly assigned to adolescents in social science studies belongs to them only as a group. As individuals, psychological commentary makes clear, they suffer uncertainty, absence of power" [Spacks, 45]). Esther's persona is clearly marked by obvious feelings of uncertainty, based on her all-too-accurate understanding that she has no power. When Buddy, who has never skiied, "instructs" Esther in the sport and encourages her in the long run that breaks her leg in two places, she obeys him mindlessly. (That she finds a sense of power in the run is an unexpected benefit for her, but in some ways a futile one: she cannot spend her life skiing.) Buddy's malevolence as he diagnoses the breaks and predicts she will be in a cast for months is a frightening insight into his true motives for maintaining their relationship while he is hospitalized. Esther is his possession, his security, his way of keeping his own self-image normal in the midst of his increasing plumpness and his morbid fear of disease.

Buddy's sadistic treatment of Esther prepares the way for the last of the New York episodes, Esther's date with the woman-hater Marco.

Replete with scenes of violence, sexual aggression, and muddy possession, this story plunges the reader further into the depravity the city has provided. Marco's brutal rape attempt and his marking Esther with blood from his bleeding nose are physically more insulting than his calling her a slut. They are also more frightening. Esther has never known such violence, such hatred, and must come to see that the man's behavior is even more frightening because it has nothing to do with her personally: Marco does not even know Esther. He coerces her into dancing so that she gives herself to his physical power; he rewards her with financial value; he in short treats her as if she were some despicable stereotyped gold digger. He sets her up. No matter how Esther behaves with Marco, however, she will become the objectionable woman he needs to punish.

Even assaulted as she is in this scene, Esther cannot react to such aggression except privately. The image of the well-behaved, modest girl shrouds her feelings, and only after she has returned to the Amazon does she make a move to reject her present life as object and victim. Carrying all her expensive clothes to the roof of the hotel, she throws them into the sky. Throwing out her clothes is a metaphor for rejecting her image as a pretty, small, and docile girl; nonetheless, her misplaced anger hurts only herself. The shock of Esther's encounter with Marco moves her past even the appearance of normality.

Dressed in borrowed clothes and still carrying Marco's blood streaks on her face, Esther returns home to be met by her mother. Unfortunately, this most caring of parents doesn't notice her daughter's visible cry for help. In the exaggeration of Plath's scene, with Mrs. Greenwood concerned only about the way Esther will take the news that she did not win a place in a writing course at Harvard, the real dilemma Esther faces in living with her family comes across vividly. For all the pretension of caring, for all the interest in the achieving-college-student daughter, for all the admiration her awards and honors have garnered, Esther's family cannot be bothered to see how distraught and strange she has become.

The same kind of denial operates through the excruciating description of Esther's physical and mental breakdown. The family's obliviousness to her behavior and appearance screams out through Esther's objectively told narration. In this section, as in the second half of the novel, set mostly in sanatoriums, Plath creates a series of role models for Esther. Esther, in turn, either approves them or discredits them. Esther's mother—both in herself and as representative of the cloying, united family—appears to think her daughter's insanity is just malingering, and is quickly discredited. The irony of Esther's life is that she must not only live in the same house with her mother but also share her bedroom, her twin beds, with the woman. Joan Gilling, a Smith student and a rival for Buddy's affections, presents the option of lesbian life, but her own stability has been irrevocably damaged and she later hangs herself. Dr. Nolan, Esther's psychiatrist, is the warm, tolerant, and just mentor whose efforts to help Esther understand herself are eventually rewarded. Nolan gives Esther permission to hate both her mother and the attitudes she represents, and to be fitted with a diaphragm, so that the previously closed—and gendered—world of sexual experience will be open to her. As Plath has presented both areas of experience throughout the book, Esther needs freeing from conventional judgments so that she will not feel so guilty about everything. One of the most telling scenes in the second half of *The Bell Jar* is Esther's reaction to her first electroconvulsive shock treatment: "I wondered what terrible thing it was that I had done" (161).

The relentless guilt Esther feels as she looks from her bedroom window and sees Dodo Conway, the pregnant neighbor wheeling her sixth child, brings all the scattered images of childbirth and woman's responsibility back into focus. Unless she accepts this role, Esther will have no life—this is the message her society, even the most supportive elements in it, gives her. But Plath has also introduced another key image during the childbirth scene, that of a "long, blind, doorless and windowless corridor of pain . . . waiting to open up and shut her in again" (72), and this image of relentless suffering recurs through the second half of the novel. It is, in fact, the title image, an encasement, unrelieved, where Esther is "stewing in my own sour air" (209). More frightening than the bewildering crotch of the fig tree, the bell jar presents no choices, no alternatives, except death. And the tone of that fearful outcome is echoed in the image of "a black, airless sack with no way out" (144). Choice has been subsumed to only guilt-ridden depression, and one of the refrains that haunts Esther in her madness is "*You'll never get anywhere like that, you'll never get anywhere like that*" (164).

The second half of *The Bell Jar* becomes a chronicle of Esther's continuing education, but an education in suicide and its various processes. So expertly and completely have the contradictions of her adolescent education been presented in the novel's first 10 chapters that Plath needs to do very little with background during the second half. Buddy Willard makes only one appearance, wondering whether it was he who drove Joan and Esther to their madness. (Esther assures him he had nothing to do with it.) Plath creates some comedy in even this macabre section, by emphasizing again what a good and diligent student Esther is. In her study of suicide, Esther reads, asks questions, correlates material, chooses according to her own personality, and progresses in expertise just as if she were writing a term paper. All factual information is given in the context of *her* needs, however, and so the essential charting of Esther's psyche becomes the second part of the novel.

Many of the episodes in the latter part of the book are skeletal. It is as if Plath were loath to give up any important details but also realized that her readers were in effect following two narratives. The first half of *The Bell Jar* gives the classic female orientation and education, with obvious indications of the failure of that education appearing during the New York experience—especially with the Marco episode and following it. The second half gives an equally classic picture of mental deterioration and its treatment, a picture relatively new to fiction in the late 1950s, significant both personally and culturally to the author. But the exigencies of the fictional form were pressing, and Plath had already crowded many characters and scenes into her brief fiction. The somewhat ambivalent ending may have occurred as much because the book was growing so long as because Plath was uncertain about the outcome of her protagonist. As the text makes clear, the main reason for the comparatively open ending lies within

Esther herself. Honest as she is, she has to remain uncertain about her health. She wonders whether the bell jar will descend again, and whether or not she would survive another depression. She sees questions ahead but also sees that she has gained a great deal of self-understanding in the process of her treatment. She affirms that leaving the asylum has been a birth, a more significant birth than the natural birth of infant from mother's womb. (Esther's throwing out the roses her mother has brought in honor of that physical birth reinforces her sense of the importance of this second birth.) As Esther says near the triumph of leaving the asylum, there should be "a ritual for being born twice" (275). The recurrence of the "old brag" of her heart—"I am, I am, I am"—is more comforting near the end of the novel than it was when it occurred earlier, in the episode in which she contemplates death through drowning.

The Esther Greenwood pictured in the later pages of *The Bell Jar* is a much more confident person. She knows she does not want to be like the lobotomized Valerie, incapable of any emotion. She knows real grief at Joan's funeral, and real anger at Buddy's condescending visit. She understands the rejection implicit in her mother's refusal to accept the truth about her illness, and the corresponding and somewhat compensatory generosity of Dr. Nolan's acceptance of it. Esther is a healthy, confident woman—and the ending scenes are even more reassuring when compared with Esther's behavior early in the novel. For the first time in the novel, she can speak directly and precisely to a man who has wronged her: "I have a bill here, Irwin," she says quietly to the man who has been her first lover. "I hate her," she admits to Dr. Nolan about her mother. "You had nothing to do with us, Buddy," she says scathingly to her former boyfriend. Even early in her breakdown, Esther is quite direct: "I can't sleep. I can't read." The irony as Plath draws these intermediary scenes is that no one will listen to Esther, no matter how clearly she speaks. Various doctors, her mother, and friends persist in translating what she is literally saying ("I haven't slept for fourteen nights") into words acceptable to them, given their views of Esther Greenwood. One climactic scene between Esther and her mother illustrates her mother's practice of mishearing and misinterpreting, and also gives the best description of the bell jar stifling Esther:

> My mother's face floated to mind, a pale reproachful moon. . . . A daughter in an asylum! I had done that to her. Still, she had obviously decided to forgive me.
>
> "We'll take up where we left off, Esther," she had said, with her sweet, martyr's smile. "We'll act as if all this were a bad dream."
>
> A bad dream.
>
> To the person in the bell jar, blank and stopped as a dead baby, the world itself is a bad dream.
>
> A bad dream.
>
> I remembered everything.
>
> I remembered the cadavers and Doreen and the story of the fig tree and Marco's diamond. . . .
>
> Maybe forgetfulness, like a kind of snow, should numb and cover them.
>
> But they were part of me. They were my landscape. (193–4)

If a woman's life must be suffused with the image of herself as nurturer, mother, passive sustainer, then the most horrible of all negative images is that of a dead baby. Plath's choice of the words *blank* and *stopped* is powerful; these words are unexpected opposites from words usually associated with a baby's growth. By implication, Esther finds herself in the dual roles of both child and mother, yet discovers no satisfaction in either. And in this scene, she finds particularly hateful the fact that her tortuous experience of madness—the most telling education she has known, an experience that has brought her to a new stage of maturity and self-understanding—is being written off by her mother as illusory, inconsequential, a bad dream. Esther's madness has been not just something to reject; it has been her means of saving herself from the pressures that a victimizing society would inflict. When Esther leaves the hospital, though she refers to herself comically as "patched, retreaded and approved for the road," her exhilaration at being free of restraint, at being truly on her own, and at being her own woman for the first time in her life is unfeigned.

Inherent in the notion of bildungsroman is the sense that any such novel will provide a blueprint for a successful education, however the word *successful* is defined. At times, as in Thomas Hardy's *Jude the Obscure*, education comes too late to save the protagonist, but the issue is more the information to be conveyed than it is the physical ending of the character's narrative. For Buckley, if the protagonist has the means to give life "some ultimate coherence," then education has been successful (Buckley, 282). *The Bell Jar* gives the reader the sense that Esther has, at least at this moment in time, gained the ability to achieve that coherence. Because so few bildungsromans deal with madness, however, exact comparisons between Plath's novel and those usually considered in the genre are difficult; nevertheless, because so many women's novels treat the subject of madness, *The Bell Jar* is no anomaly. Its very representativeness is suggested in Spacks's comment that most female novels of adolescence "stress the world's threat more than its possibilities; their happy endings derive less from causal sequence than from fortunate accident" (Spacks, 120). The titles of comparable novels indicate this difference. *The Bell Jar*, with its somewhat sinister implications of airlessness, imprisonment, and isolation, is a far remove from Charles Dickens's *Great Expectations*, the language of which suggests immeasurable promise. And in its most positive scenes, *The Bell Jar* cannot approach the ringing self-confidence of James Joyce's *A Portrait of the Artist as a Young Man*, which has its own imagery of figs and choices, though it is surely that novel writ female.

Among other differences between (a) the conventional bildungsroman that deals with a young man's education and (b) the female novel of experience in adolescence is the shift in the role of crucial parent from father to mother. Because much of the process of education is imitative, figures that serve as role models also shift from male to female. A female bildungsroman will thus seem to be peopled more heavily with women characters than with men although cultural imperatives will keep the latter—economically, socially, and sexually— prominent. It may be because men must occur in these female novels that they are often viewed as adversaries or antagonists, whereas in the male bildungsroman women characters can simply be omitted.

Educational experiences and choices leading to occupations will also differ, but none will be quite so persuasive as the female's need to choose between profession and domesticity. The inescapability of this choice forces many a novel that might be labeled bildungsroman into the category of the less prestigious domestic novel. Underlying what would seem to be the choice of profession is the less visible issue of sexuality, which again plays a very different role in female versus male adolescence. In the conventional novel of education, sexual experience is just another step toward maturity; it provides a means for the male character to exchange one household for another. For a man, such a move may mean only that he hangs his coat in a different closet. For a woman, however, the move away from the family home means a complete change of status, from mistress to servant—that is, to the person responsible for the housekeeping in ways she would never have been as a daughter of her father's house.

A parallel loss of status occurs in sexual maturity. Biological necessity and physical size mean that the female is a more passive partner in intercourse. The accoutrements of a sexual relationship—because so much social and economic currency depends on that relationship for women—differ for women. Losing one's virginity unwisely seldom determines the entire life of a male character, whereas it is the stuff of ostracism, abortion, madness, or suicide for the female. Plath's concern with Esther's sexual experience is relevant, for Esther's choices will determine her future. Her aggression in finding Irwin so that she can be sexually experienced is positive, but Plath's pervasive irony—that Esther's first intercourse is marred by the frightening vaginal tear—foreshadows the bad luck that often follows such a reversal of cultural roles. As Plath knew, society had its means of punishing women who were too aggressive, too competent, or too masculine.

The apparent connections between the author's experiences and the characters' are legitimate topics of discussion where bildungsromans are concerned because the strength of such novels usually depends on the writer's emotional involvement with them. The bildungsroman is often an early novel—a first or second one—and much of the life, as well as the ambivalence, of the novel exists because the author is so heavily invested in the narrative. Plath's *The Bell Jar* was her first novel, and it was also a partly disguised statement of her anger toward a culture and a family that would accept her only provided that she did "acceptable" things. Because this tone of wrenching anger makes *The Bell Jar* seem different from the novels usually categorized as bildungsromans, critics have seldom placed it in that category. The wry self-mockery that gives way to the cryptic poignance of Esther's madness has no antecedent in earlier novels of development. It is in tone and mood that Plath succeeded in making the conventional form—which she followed in a number of important respects—her own.

The narrative *The Bell Jar* ultimately told was of a woman struggling to become whole, not that of a woman who had reached some sense of a stable self. That conclusion, according to Annis Pratt in her study *Archetypal Patterns in Women's Fiction*, is what any reader might expect from a talented and aware woman writer. As Pratt observes, "even the most conservative women authors create narratives manifesting an acute tension between what any normal human being might desire and what a woman must become. Women's fiction reflects an experience radically different from men's because our drive towards growth as persons is thwarted by our society's prescriptions concerning gender. . . . [W]e are outcasts in the land." So far as the generic differences are concerned, then, the female hero in a woman's bildungsroman will be "destined for disappointment." Pratt concludes, "The vitality and hopefulness characterizing the adolescent hero's attitude toward her future here meet and conflict with the expectations and dictates of the surrounding society. Every element of her desired world—freedom to come and go, allegiance to nature, meaningful work, exercise of the intellect, and use of her own erotic capabilities—inevitably clashes with patriarchal norms" (Pratt, 5–6).

The Bell Jar must certainly be read as the story of that inevitable clash, a dulled and dulling repetition of lives all too familiar to contemporary readers; and a testimony to the repressive cultural mores that trapped many midcentury women, forcing them outside what should have been their rightful, productive lives.

7

The Bell Jar and the Patriarchy

Except for Buddy Willard, there appear to be very few male characters in Plath's novel. On second glance, however, there are men at every turn, and they are often the characters who control the direction of the narrative, the women characters, and eventual outcomes. While much of the characterization of separate male figures is scant and scattered, Plath locates them within a culture that itself endows them with power. Cal, her beach date, or Constantin, the U.N. interpreter, are vivid embodiments of male sexuality; they represent the patriarchy in all its erotic, financial, and domestic power.

The primary structure of the patriarchy is a male head (of household or church or school, etc.) distributing power on the basis of tribal "law." Whether or not that law is based on primogeniture, men usually see that most of the power passes to other men. Within Plath's novelistic world, the male head of household—Esther's father—is absent, yet his early and unexpected death gives him power through his family's memory. Part of Esther's pervasive guilt stems from her belief that she never managed to please her father; more of it stems from her failure to adequately mourn his death. Her atonement as she finds and visits his grave is part of her preparation for suicide.

Because she has no father, Esther places great importance on her relationships with boyfriends. She seems to give her beaux the authority of the combined roles of father and future husband. To the relatively normal eagerness of an adolescent searching for her husband-to-be Esther adds her need for fathering. Within the narrative, Plath shows Esther's dependence by giving her physical hungers that her boyfriends fill, as when Constantin feeds her and Buddy and Cal instruct her.

With the exception of Jay Cee in New York, all the teaching in *The Bell Jar* is done by men. Mr. Manzi, Esther's physics teacher, runs a difficult class, using her straight-A record to quiet complaints about the course from other women students. The old doctor at the sanatorium teaches Esther about pilgrims, even though she is reasonably more interested in her own mental health. Buddy defines himself almost entirely by what he can find to explain to Esther, from scientific and medical matters through the infamous skiing lesson and sex to his learning about poetry and other literary matters. Buddy takes all knowledge as his province, but Plath suggests that his inquiry is important chiefly as a way to give himself authority in relation to other people. Cal instructs Esther in the methods of suicide, though his own lack of physical prowess as they swim undercuts his authority. (The name Cal, with its suggestion of both Caliban and Caligula, becomes sinister in conjunction with Plath's choice of the name Ariel. It also suggests Robert Lowell's nickname of Cal, and in his arrogance and insensitivity, Plath may have been thinking of the established poet whose course she audited in Boston during winter 1959 in Boston (Axelrod, 66–67). While Esther continues swimming and Cal returns to the beach, she visualizes him as one of many white worms, "lost . . . among dozens and dozens of other worms that were wriggling or just lolling about between the sea and the sky" (131).

The patriarchy and its pervasive misuse of power are best represented in the characters of (a) Marco, the abusive woman-hater whose interaction with Esther is scarifying, and (b) the seemingly much more respectable Dr. Gordon, the self-important psychiatrist whose abuse of Esther occurs in the malfunctioning of the electroconvulsive shock he administers to her as an outpatient. With no second opinion and little prior talk, Gordon's shock treatments—bipolar, given without adequate preparation or follow-up counseling—are disastrous. No sooner does the treatment begin than August arrives, and Gordon goes on vacation, referring Esther to a colleague.

"By the roots of my hair some god got hold of me. / I sizzled in his blue volts" is a description from a later Plath poem.[26] Esther, as Plath describes her, feels intense pain. She is frightened beyond the words available to her at this point in her depression. Although her mother has told her the treatment will make her well, it is doing nothing of the kind, and Esther's resentment at her mother's advice is a source of her later anger.

Plath's description of Dr. Gordon is scathing. A "pretty" man, he values appearance—and the reader surmises that Esther, in her unkempt, sleepless, and dirty state, does not interest him. He fails to listen to her and in fact quotes her mother's opinions to her instead of asking her questions directly (e.g., "Your mother tells me you are upset"). The doctor Esther labels as "conceited" and "arrogant" then asks her, condescendingly, "Suppose you try and tell me what you think is wrong." Esther's reaction is correct: she becomes angry. His use of the word *try* suggests that she will not be able to tell him anything, and the rest of the sentence, in Esther's words, is as follows:

> I turned the words over suspiciously, like round, sea-polished pebbles that might suddenly put out a claw and change into something else.
>
> What did I *think* was wrong?
>
> That made it sound as if nothing was *really* wrong, I only *thought* it was wrong. (105–6)

In answer to her description of her state of mind, Dr. Gordon seems to listen and to think, but then he makes some inappropriate comment about his having been the doctor for a WAVE or WAC troup housed at her college during World War II. Nothing in his comment has any bearing on Esther's problems, and she has the feeling he could have made this observation without either seeing or hearing her.

At a second session a week later, when Esther again describes the symptoms that by now are worse, Dr. Gordon seems to listen once more. This time, however, he makes no comment to her but instead asks to see her mother, to whom he suggests the shock treatments. Esther's continuing feeling of alienation from the psychiatrist who should be her chief support at this time undoubtedly damages the treatments' effectiveness. Plath emphasizes that Esther is in the hands of an uncaring physician, and that the outcome of her treatment will only further augment the depression she is already experiencing.

The damage the patriarchal system has done to Esther, as Plath describes it in *The Bell Jar*, is both real and frequent. It is a physical and an emotional reality. Buddy's ski instruction causes Esther to break her leg severely and to live in a hip cast the entire semester of her junior year in college. Marco's violence—calling her names, hitting her, throwing her in the mud, attempting rape—is as damaging emotionally as it is physically. Esther's leaving his blood streaks across her cheeks is her visible expression of her fear, anger, and dismay. Ironically, Esther's mother comprehends neither what the blood is nor what it might signify. And Dr. Gordon's damage through the "electrocution" of his treatment seems irrevocable.

Though only suggested, Esther's emotional damage from the erstwhile abandonment of her father through his unexpected death is one of the causes of her breakdown. And the sexual narrative, which the scenes with Buddy, Lenny Shepherd, and Marco build so effectively, culminates with Irwin's cavalier complacency about both Esther's pain and her bleeding. As the literal instrument of her wounding, Irwin offers no caring behavior, no human concern, no sympathy. For all the biological intimacy of the act of sexual intercourse, making love with Irwin is an isolating experience: Esther is no longer a virgin, but she is as alone as she has ever been.

Most of the damage to Esther occurs because of the laws the patriarchal system enforces. In the case of Marco, society would say that Esther is not dating suitable people and therefore "deserves" whatever happens (the tie with Doreen and Lenny would be emphasized). In the situation with Irwin, Esther is so totally at fault for having sex outside wedlock that she has no recourse against Irwin's stolid indifference. In the case of Buddy, Esther's duty as his girlfriend is to listen and to obey. And in the case of Dr. Gordon, society's assumption is that a medical man should have full authority over troubled women's lives. Just as Dr. Gordon treats Esther in such a manner as to bring on her depressive reaction and her eventual suicide attempt, so he replaces the distant and uncaring father figure of her imagination. Mixed with Esther's anger at what she knows to be Dr. Gordon's mistreatment of her is her own childhood guilt at having caused her sick father trouble, at not playing her role as good girl suitably.

For Plath to write a novel that even attempts to end happily, she must focus more heavily on women characters, on Esther in roles through which she can succeed without great attention from the very men who have been the cause of her wounding in the first place. Accordingly, from the time of the scenes with Dr. Gordon there are few men who appear in *The Bell Jar*. Buddy makes only a few cameo appearances; Constantin and Cal disappear forever, as does Dr. Gordon; and Esther herself is far removed from the state of mind in which she cares about attracting boyfriends. After her swimming date with Cal, Esther avoids all boys. She does not feel up to meeting or dating any of them, because they pose the biggest challenge to her future life: if she is to marry someone worthy, then she must attract some man of that caliber.

Plath's real brilliance in crafting *The Bell Jar* is in having a number of the older women characters become spokespeople for the patriarchal view. Although Mrs. Willard is the clearest example of a woman's speaking those male-identified truths, many other characters fill the same roles, even if less visibly. When Esther complains so brusquely about "these weird old women," her reader shares that feeling. Not self-sufficient women, not women who have chosen to put their careers and their desires first, but women who inscribe their words and actions in the power of the patriarchal realm, many of the women characters in *The Bell Jar* have sold out to the enemy in countless ways. Esther counts them: "There was the famous poet, and Philomena Guinea, and Jay Cee, and the Christian Scientist lady and lord knows who, and they all wanted to adopt me in some way, and, for the price of their care and influence, have me resemble them" (180). For these women characters, as for the traditional male, Esther exists to be shaped. Her surname, Greenwood, is a signal that she will be malleable, pliant, and ready to respond to the first authoritative voice she hears. The famous poet is scandalized when Esther tells her she wants to marry and have children: "But what about your *career*?" the poet cries. Esther's mother yearns for the dutiful, virginal daughter she has known in earlier times; she does not want Esther to grow up and away from her. Philomena Guinea will help Esther during her breakdown only if no boy is involved in her depression. And in the midst of these conflicting directives, Esther must make decisions that affect both her life and her mental and physical health. The fig tree metaphor of choices impossible to make is inaccurate only because it is a less complex image than would accurately represent the dilemma Esther faces.

While the novel's older women characters speak for the patriarchy, the younger women either mimic their elders, as does Dodo Conway, or become unwomanly in their professionalism. Jay Cee becomes an object of ridicule to the smart young college women of the College Board because, even though she has power on the magazine, she dresses unstylishly and seems unfeminine. So far as Esther's role is concerned, she is left without adequate models. Part of Esther's hatred for her mother stems from the fact that Mrs. Greenwood has been co-opted by the patriarchal laws that stifle women's ambition and desire, not to mention their sexuality. Mrs. Greenwood has subordinated her life to her husband's and, even though her life has been used up in his, thinks it perfectly suitable for Esther to do the same for the man she marries. The reason Esther's choices of men to date are so crucial, of such interest to her mother, is the assumption that Esther too will live through her husband. Mrs. Willard and Dodo Conway have made the same decisions and serve to reify Mrs. Greenwood's role in the novel.

Rather than deal directly with the issue of modeling for Esther, Plath focuses on the loss of her father and, more important, on her mother's role of keeping Esther from mourning his death. An archetypal competition between mother and daughter over the male beloved brings Esther to attest, "I had always been my father's favorite, and it seemed fitting I should take on a mourning my mother had never bothered with" (135). Esther's hostility toward her mother and toward the woman's response to her husband's death is seldom spoken; outwardly, Esther is her mother's very life and seems appreciative of the many sacrifices her martyrlike mother insists on making for her well-being. Like anger, hostility is unseemly, inappropriate. Like sexual expression, venting rage must be handled carefully, circumspectly, within the boundaries of moral behavior. And just as a young woman does not have sex outside marriage, so a daughter does not criticize the mother who has given her everything in life. The issue of Esther's burgeoning understanding that she is hostile toward Mrs. Greenwood becomes the subtext of *The Bell Jar*. The novel is a book about mothers and daughters as well as a study of one young woman's psychic break-down and recovery; in fact, the primary theme may be the former.

Plath shows the interrelationship of these themes through several carefully structured scenes. The climactic scene in which Esther searches for, and finally finds, her father's grave works for several purposes. Esther is mourning not only the loss of her father but the loss of his memory, the fact that she has been carefully shut out of the process of both knowing him and grieving for his loss. Even though the scene is about Esther's finding her father's grave, it also describes by implication Mrs. Greenwood's role in keeping Esther from her father, even from any knowledge of his impending death. The focus in Plath's text as Esther walks through the cemetery moves from the ostensible search for the father's grave to a less well articulated search for her own sorrow, her own spiritual center, the capacity to feel grief. The despair that has fueled Esther's search and, the reader presumes, her breakdown is flooded away in the cleansing of her tears. Once Esther has reclaimed that human grief (which is, again, set against the contrasting bland and stoic acceptance her mother shows over that death), has become once more the child of her father as well as of her mother, she is able to act. Esther's decision to kill herself comes almost as a positive turn, especially because it follows weeks of indecision.

For much of the time, however, Esther is incapable of acting in any way. She thinks comparatively unwholesome and surprising thoughts, particularly about the older women trying to influence her life. Esther's relationships with these women are her means of defining herself and of defying the conservative older generation. One expects generational warfare, particularly in fiction with a college-age protagonist; thus, what is often the generational struggle in *The Bell Jar* seems antifemale. Esther's hostile responses to the women who have been her mentors, friends, relatives, and employers are less critical than they might appear, once they are viewed in the perspective of generational difference.

Esther's hatred of the older women is in some respects a continuation of the deep taboo she has already expressed by admitting she is angry about her father's death. The daughter's role in the family relationship—the daughter's only role in most Western cultures—is to wait for the benediction of the father. Because of the fear of incest, the father must distance himself from his daughter—and so he ignores her, treats her as subordinate, different in kind and responsibility from her brothers. A passive charity is the best the loved daughter can hope for.

Being competitive, an ambitious daughter would be angry from the start at this treatment. In *The Bell Jar*, however, because Plath relegates Esther's father to the role of the absent one, Esther's anger at his absence makes little rational sense; instead, Plath shows Esther's need to mourn her father's absence and death. But what actually is happening in Esther's mind is that someone deserves her anger, and while it is—as she has consistently been taught—unseemly for her to be angry with her dead father, there is little stigma attached to her being angry with her living mother. (Indeed, there is some precedent for this anger, because one of the cultural patterns of the 1950s was anger or distaste toward the female parent.) The plausible explanation for Esther's anger lies in the fact that it is displaced—is directed at the patriarchy and all its control—yet is expressed toward these hovering and seemingly well-intentioned older women who, through their example and language, reconfirm the teaching of that patriarchy.

8

The Bell Jar as Economic Text

Too often, readers of the 1960s, 1970s, 1980s, and 1990s have had difficulty understanding the comparatively rigid social stratification in place during the increasingly prosperous 1940s and 1950s. The 1930s decade of depression created a society acutely conscious of material wealth, and survivors of that period of unexpected and omnipresent financial disaster tended to live their lives as conspicuous consumers. If people had wealth, they showed it.

In *The Bell Jar*, Plath depicts a typical economic paradigm: most of the women attending Smith College are wealthy. They have in common such things as summer homes on Cape Cod, cars, expensive clothes, and prep school experiences. They choose boyfriends who attended Ivy League schools, matching their Seven Sisters pedigree with that of their male counterparts. In short, by the means of many cultural and social signs, these women "belong."

In contrast to these typical college women who accept attending this fashionable and elite women's college as their right, Esther Greenwood—as the modestly middle-class scholarship student she is—must be content with never belonging. Nothing Esther does will ever make her a part of the "in" crowd. These socially accepted women have known one another through the tennis-tournament-riding-show-private-academy-elite-summer-camp circuits, not to mention contacts among parents and families whose wealth brings them into even greater proximity. They have no reason to take Esther into their social circle. She does not belong; she will not belong; she will never belong—unless she marries one of their men. Esther's staying on in Northampton to buy clothes on sale during vacations (from the expensive shops the other students patronize regularly, paying full prices) is symptomatic of her outsider status.

Plath makes clear that Esther Greenwood is not a "loner" by choice. Repeatedly, Esther tries to play the connections game—she finds Buddy Willard desirable largely because he goes to Yale; she is willing to baby-sit for the summer so that she can be somewhere on the Cape and therefore near people who customarily summer there; and part of her defeat the summer of her depression comes from having to stay home with her family. Without an awareness of the social and financial mores of the 1950s, readers might attribute the importance of these events to Esther's tendency to depression rather than to the lockstep economic/class situation within U.S. society.

Economic considerations make Esther's need to marry well much more than just a personally motivated dream. In the 1950s women's social and financial standing depended almost entirely on their husbands' occupation. If a woman did work, it was thought of as self-fulfillment rather than for monetary gain. Women's occupations were secondary to those of their husbands, and readily dispensable. The pattern of working awhile after college, and even after marriage, only to leave the work force once children were born—and returning only after those children were in college, perhaps 20 years later—was the common one. Women's professional needs were thought to be supplied by the roles of wife, housekeeper, and mother; few women could admit to being emotionally interested in their work. When they did return to working outside the home once their children were older, the demands of their family remained primary.

One of the greatest ironies in *The Bell Jar* is having the thoroughly desirable Buddy Willard (ideal husband material because of his education at Yale, his considerable eventual earning power, his respectable and well-educated family, and his personal ambition) say tactlessly about Esther that she will have difficulty marrying now that she has been institutionalized. He inquires of her, however, whom she will (choose to) marry, now that she has been institutionalized, which darkens the tone of his comment to insult. His question assumes that to Esther's qualities of near poverty, extreme intelligence, height, and overintense personality she has voluntarily added the fact of her breakdown and institutionalization. Willard's question ignores the real dynamics of power during the 1950s, when women waited to be asked by men who wished to marry them. Like other 1950s women, Esther Greenwood would have to be content with waiting until some man asked her to marry him, and knowing her medical history would make such a proposal unlikely. The distancing Buddy Willard achieves by his phrasing, given that he himself has earlier proposed to Esther, is scathingly clear. Plath's setting him in the foolish role of man-who-needs-help-from-woman as Esther digs out his car does little to reverse the power roles, though that is probably one of Plath's intentions in the scene.

Another quality of Esther's character that is a direct result of social and economic pressures during the 1950s is her gratefulness. She has been reminded so often that she is the benefactor of other people's generosity that she assumes the role of the thankful woman in nearly every scene. Because of her training in gratefulness, Esther finds it difficult to become angry. Instead of anger, she often feels guilty for what she does or does not do—when, as Plath's text shows so clearly, Esther has very little real choice in her life. She is the victim of economic and social mores, of her mother's continual (and unrealistic) prodding to make her even more thankful than she already is, and of her own thoroughly ingrained sense of personal inadequacy. The reason Dr. Nolan brings to Esther—and the text—the freshness of real emotion is that no one else in the novel acts on feelings. Mrs. Greenwood is so cushioned round with what people will think or say, with what is proper for the decently middle class who are being given educations and jobs, that she cannot act spontaneously. Unfortunately, she has also lost her power to hear what her daughter is saying, and is of no aid at all when Esther is in emotional jeopardy.

The juxtaposition of scenes and dialogue segments within the novel plainly shows Plath's intention to present Esther's mother as the victim of social beliefs about women that are harmful to her development and her daughter's. While Plath makes clear the pragmatic philosophy that directs Mrs. Greenwood's life—counting her accomplishments in terms of jobs done and money saved—the reader can maintain some sympathy for her in certain sections of the book: after all, she is the sole support of her family. But by the time of Esther's analysis with Dr. Nolan, it becomes clear that much of Esther's psychological difficulty stems from the demands her mother makes of her. Esther remembers only one reaction from her mother to her institutionalization: "My mother's face floated to mind, a pale, reproachful moon, at her last and first visit to the asylum since my twentieth birthday" (193).

Unrelieved guilt at the trouble she has caused her mother is one of Esther's primary emotions. Another is fear that she will be found out, discovered to be not worthy of the benefits her society has given her (another lesson her mother has taught her well). The night nurse who moonlights in the elite institution as well as working at the "state place" during the day throws Esther into a panic as she suggests Esther might be more suitable for the state institution. Calling her "Lady Jane," in some strange intertextual play on D. H. Lawrence's *Lady Chatterley's Lover*, the brusque nurse says flatly, "You wouldn't like it over there one bit. . . . [I]t's not a nice place, like this. This is a regular country club. Over there they've got nothing. No OT to talk of, no walks. . . . Not enough em-ploy-ees" (170). The difference between the care money can buy, even though the personnel providing the care is the same, reinscribes economic considerations on Esther's consciousness. She is indebted not to her mother but to the older writer, her mentor at Smith, Philomena Guinea, for her care and analysis in this "country club" private institution. The economic dialogue continues as the mention of a country club signals Esther's grandfather's job as headwaiter in a local country club, another reminder of her outsider status in the social circles of her community.

The Bell Jar *as Economic Text*

When the scene with Mrs. Greenwood's bringing Esther roses for her birthday is viewed as a segment of the carefully constructed economic statement, it gains even more poignance. Esther's mother is already exhausted financially. She cannot take on any more work—she already teaches summer school and has no capacity to teach elsewhere—but her income is limited and constant. Unexpected expenses like Esther's medical care, as well as the possibility of continuing psychological care, leave her desperate. She simply has no resources. Luckily, Philomena Guinea has come to the rescue, financially and psychologically. But her generosity only makes both Mrs. Greenwood and Esther even more indebted to the system, and to her as its benefactor. Thus, for Esther's mother to purchase roses, the most expensive of the hothouse flowers, is an extravagance she cannot afford, and when that gesture is so thoroughly rebuffed, as Esther throws the flowers in the wastebasket, Mrs. Greenwood is devastated. The importance of this scene, as Plath creates it in her narrative, is not so much that the scene happens as that it provides a text for Esther's session with Dr. Nolan. Telling her about it, Esther announces, "That was a silly thing for her to do." Dr. Nolan agrees, deflecting the reader who has been thinking that throwing the roses away was a "silly thing" for Esther to have done, perhaps a needlessly hurtful thing for her to have done to her mother. But as a result of both her action and her retelling of it to Dr. Nolan, Esther can then say, for the first time, "I hate her." Unsure of her doctor's reaction to this unprecedentedly naughty statement, Esther, adds the narrative, "waited for the blow to fall." But Esther—and the reader—is reassured because Dr. Nolan understands that Esther's coming to anger over her mother's behavior is necessary, and the ending of the scene is triumphant: "But Doctor Nolan only smiled at me as if something had pleased her very, very much, and said, 'I suppose you do'" (166).

In careful fragments, Plath creates a completely positive persona for Dr. Nolan, who gains force as the only strong yet humane woman character in the novel because her role regarding Esther is to empower her. Through Nolan's encouragement, Esther is made to understand what her abilities are, why she responds as she does, and why her responses are normal. The problems with Esther's adjusting to the world are that other older people in her world are themselves restricted and, accordingly, attempt to restrict her in her patterns of growth and exploration. But Nolan avoids being either judgmental or simplistic: she lets Esther know what the struggle is and why it is crucial to Esther's eventual health. Contrary to most of the characters in *The Bell Jar*, Dr. Nolan speaks rarely and with curious simplicity: "Tell me about Doctor Gordon. Did you like him?" and "I'm going over with you. I'll be there the whole time, so everything will happen right, the way I promised. I'll be there when you wake up, and I'll bring you back again" (155, 173). Confident yet confidential, Dr. Nolan is depicted as the ideal practitioner of psychoanalysis.

Not only does Dr. Nolan provide Esther with the confidence and understanding to heal herself, but she acts as a caregiver in the fullest sense of the word. When Esther has her electroconvulsive shock treatments, it is Dr. Nolan who wakes her and draws her back into life. When Joan commits suicide, it is Dr. Nolan who explains that suicide is no one's fault, least of all Esther's. And it is Dr. Nolan who gives Esther the courage to come before the examining board so that she can be released and return to college. Without relying on explicit imagery or scenes, Plath creates the woman psychiatrist as Esther's mother figure, and the respect and love Esther has thought might be placed in Jay Cee, as the successful professional writer, is finally given to Dr. Nolan.

The alternatives to Esther's behavior in the sanatorium are represented by the personae of Valerie, passive and calm after her lobotomy, and Miss Harris, whose catatonic nonspeaking contrasts with Esther's comparative volubility. In the case of Valerie, the operation has got rid of the haunting anger that marked her emotional life. Esther's anger, in contrast, needs to be developed and spoken. Climactic scenes with Dr. Nolan are those about Esther's throwing her mother's roses away; being able to say she hates her mother; and expressing her fears of sex. In the case of Miss Harris, whose closed lips are roselike but grotesque in their silence, Esther's attempts to help her, to bring her to speech, are important indices of her caring nature. The respective failures of the maimed Valerie and the catatonic Miss Harris contrast vividly with Esther's eventual health—and even more vividly with Joan Gilling's suicide. Even in the most expensive of institutions, no one can predict what kind of results patients will experience. That Esther could be cared for in such an expensive place helps allow her anger to crystallize: there is a cost for the "help" that her mother and her mother's friends give, and Esther finds herself tired of having to pay— and pay, and pay—for guilts and angers she developed quite naturally. As a sentient woman living amid the powerful patriarchy, herself powerless economically, Esther could not blink away the problems that being female—and relatively poor—caused.

Being from the middle-class, educated, elite white Boston community, Esther yet remains an outsider for economic and gender reasons. She does not have the money for the accoutrements her culture expects—pretty and fashionable clothes, a car, money for travel and for advanced degrees from good schools. Being female, she is destined to be an economic parasite, living off her husband's earnings and being relegated to the role of helpmeet, to spend her life's value in such small economies as Mrs. Willard's picnic lunches and woven kitchen rugs.

Yet every event in *The Bell Jar* shows the reader Esther's brilliance and promise. The structure of the book assures the reader that Esther can do anything a man her age can. She has perfect grades; she has won prizes for many years; she works hard and earns a lot of her own money; she is ambitious, prudent, talented, mannerly—and so enraged she cannot live healthily on this earth. The continuous subjection that has been her life experience has finally broken through, and the narrative she writes is one means of her expressing that accumulated rage. Even though the opening of the novel is reassuring—Esther has married and has had a child; she is cutting off the starfish to make a toy for it—most of the text explores the anger Esther learns to know once she has accepted her role in her culture: penniless, powerless, and female. It is no accident that in the same year *The Bell Jar* appeared, Betty Friedan's *The Feminine Mystique*—the study of women's anger and possible solutions to it—saw print. The role of talented yet powerless women would become a major theme in the social history of the United States for the next decades.

9

The Double in *The Bell Jar*

Frequently in her writing, Plath turns to a theme that had fascinated her from college days. Her honors thesis at Smith College was titled "The Magic Mirror: A Study of the Double in Two of Dostoevsky's Novels." Reading Otto Rank, Frazer, Jung, Nietzsche, and others, Plath plunged into the study of what she called "all fascinating stuff about the ego as symbolized in reflections (mirror and water), shadows, twins."[27]

Her thesis was undertaken the year after her breakdown and semester of convalescence, and because Plath used her scholarly talents to learn as much as possible about her own mental situation, she had become interested in what the "self" meant, ways society viewed that self, and strategies people adopted to explore their own psyches under the guise of studying other kinds of personalities. With the careful pragmatism that marked much of her life, Plath typically invested her study in her art (when she was researching modern painting, for example, she wrote a number of poems about paintings). What Plath found in the fiction of Dostoyevsky was the willingness to bare the truth of human emotion, with all its contradictions, complexities, and darknesses. What she found in studying the psychological necessity of the double—of recognizing within another the very traits one might not want to recognize under self-scrutiny—was a means of dealing with the fact that Sylvia Plath experienced a number of conflicting and sometimes-frightening beliefs about life and her role in it. Her choice to be an independent woman writer or scholar, rather than the place from which the "arrow" (the male whose life she, as a woman, was destined to support) shot off meant that she was reinforcing her sense of difference, that she was exacerbating the isolation she had already experienced too often in her life. Her choice of profession guaranteed that she would lead a life of divided consciousness.

After her work on the thesis, which she wrote under the direction of a young professor of Russian, George Gibian, Plath could react positively to Dostoyevsky's challenging task, drawing the dark night of the soul so that readers could empathize with the pained characters he had created. As she wrote in the conclusion of her study, "Although the figure of the Double has become a harbinger of danger and destruction, taking form as it does from the darkest of human fears and repressions, Dostoevsky implied that recognition of our various mirror images and reconciliation with them will save us from disintegration."[28] Plath's trying to face the natural human conflict—and, by writing about it both in her fiction and in her thesis, to work her way through it, to explore rather than dismiss that conflict and thereby to survive it—is the mark of psychological bravery that colors her oeuvre as writer. The late poems, along with *The Bell Jar*, are the most striking results of that undertaking. Her investigation into the self caught in an unquestionable—and perhaps unresolvable—dilemma is probably the quality that led Arthur Oberg, in his study of the contemporary lyric, to describe Plath as "perhaps a poet who lived and wrote almost before what might have been her time."[29] Oberg's statement reminds the reader that the pervasive mode of the 1950s was denial, not questioning or exploration.

Such a view of Plath leads to Anne Cluysenaar's image of Plath as "a typical 'survivor' in the psychiatric sense. Her work shows many traits which are recognized as marking the psychology of those who have, in some bodily or psychic sense, survived an experience of death

. . . extreme vulnerability to danger. As an element in this complex of emotions, imagining death has a life-enhancing function. It is an assertion of power, over death but also (less attractive but psychologically authentic) over other human beings." Cluysenaar concludes, "That is the crux of her message—the retention of discrimination and the will to speak, the will to communicate. Her determination not to accept relief from any ready-made dogma is admirable."[30]

Being privy to the unpublished Plath letters, especially those written in the early 1960s, when she was writing *The Bell Jar*, confirms Cluysenaar's sense of the anguish, not to mention the anger, Plath had survived. But her work itself and her comments about it show that instead of "dogma," she had rooted herself in art, and that her sense of herself had sprung from her knowledge of that art and of her own important role in its development.

For all her recognition of the angst of being an artist in America—a fairly traditional literary role in the past 200 years of American literary history—Plath never created a permanent double figure. She instead tried to avoid separating personal self from artistic self, insisting that a woman's life can contain the ingredients for an artistic, imaginative life. Plath believed that the deepest encounters with life could occur in daily experiences that were marked with their own kind of spirituality, the spirituality of self-knowledge.

Plath's notion that the writerly life evolved from the writer's daily existence depended in part on the model she had found in the work of Virginia Woolf. As Steven Axelrod claims in his recent study, *The Bell Jar* is in some ways a revision of Woolf's *Mrs. Dalloway*, despite all the apparent differences. Although Clarissa Dalloway struggles against the hatred for her culture that Esther Greenwood comes to find healthful, the works have the same roots: *The Bell Jar*, Axelrod maintains, "undertakes to retell and to revise Mrs. Dalloway's fundamental story: it examines a woman's place, choices, and suffering in a patriarchal culture, posing self-annihilation as one possible antidote to pain. . . . [B]oth Clarissa and Esther mutely anticipate suicide and then eloquently reflect on it, Clarissa when she learns of the death of her double, Septimus Smith" (Axelrod, 113).

The Double in The Bell Jar

While Axelrod may push too insistently on the intertextuality of *The Bell Jar*, his emphasis is on the fact that "both Clarissa and Esther symbolically undergo their death by means of a double, who represents, enacts, and purges their suicidal impulse" (Axelrod, 121). In *The Bell Jar*, Esther's double appears relatively late but then dominates the last fifth of the book. Joan Gilling takes over Esther's narrative and in some ways does displace the central protagonist: she is the only other woman character present in the second half of the novel with any consistency, and—unlike Doreen and Betsy from the New York scene—Joan is complex enough to mirror Esther's psychological states. The reader understands that for Esther to mimic either Doreen or Betsy is, finally, not an important choice; they are so easily categorized—stereotyped, in fact—that they do not serve as any real way to understand Esther. In Joan's case, there are more similarities as to motive, life choices, ability, and outcomes.

Joan's characterization exists chiefly to allow Plath to explore the theme of the double, and particularly the theme of the gifted and wealthy eastern woman. Joan is the more classic women's college student, the more typical Seven Sisters product than the poorer and more alienated Esther Greenwood. Joan "belongs" more much readily than Esther does. Battles are not daily duties; rather, they are encounters to be chosen for some point. Getting up every day and putting on clothes that seem different, that mark Esther as the outsider, is not one of Joan's problems.

Joan is so traditional a women's college student that in places she provides comic relief. Just as Doreen is a heavily fictionalized persona of the pliant southern sexpot—bearing little resemblance to the *Mademoiselle* College Board editor that was her point of origin—so Joan is a fantasy of the prep school product who had every advantage money could buy. Joan rides: she has access to the horses she so transparently resembles. For Plath, the costs of horses and riding, like those of boats and sailing, were too high to ever be a part of her life. Riding was an integral part of private schooling and summer camp activity, and the life of the horsewoman was filled with visible cultural markers—costumes, practice hours, lessons, shows—that excluded peers not engaged in the same sport. There was no way for a friend to be a hanger-on to the riding circle.

Joan's chief characteristic, then, sets her at an extreme financial distance from Esther, and her frequent association with horses becomes a way of reinforcing the picture of both her advantaged life and Esther's comparatively poor one. Moreover, Joan represents the wealthy elite in several other respects, those less likely to be seen as stock characteristics. Joan is a character who has the luxury of *choice*: few women characters in Plath's work have that luxury. Descriptions of Joan stress that she *chooses* to do this or that; unlike Esther, she is not coerced by society, family, or economy to make appropriate decisions.

Introduced early in the novel as Esther's competition for Buddy Willard (he comes to see Esther while he is at Smith for the sophomore prom, at the invitation of Joan), Joan is negatively described (and even in that early description, connected with the equestrian): "Joan Gilling came from our home town and went to our church and was a year ahead of me at college. She was a big wheel—president of her class and a physics major and the college hockey champion. She always made me feel squirmy with her starey pebble-colored eyes and her gleaming tombstone teeth and her breathy voice. She was big as a horse, too" (48). Leadership, the proper intellectually demanding scientific major, athletics—Joan is the 1950s dream, a woman who can handle "men's roles." In this *Sputnik*-dominated era, women who majored in English or the humanities were slotted into pink ghettos of employment even before graduation. Mrs. Greenwood's worries about Esther's needing shorthand to get a job are not unfounded. But what Plath does with these decidedly favorable qualities is to subvert them by describing Joan's lack of beauty—"starey" eyes, "tombstone" teeth, and a "horsey" build were not the requisites of the 1950s Audrey Hepburn idealization of femininity.

Further negative qualifications follow: Joan's mother has arranged the date with Buddy, through his mother. Buddy's response to going out with Joan adds to the negative description: she is a cheap date, not caring whether he spends money, and she is able to hold her own on bike trips, not needing Buddy's help up hills. Again, setting Joan at such variance with the decade's assessment of womanly characteristics serves two purposes. First, Esther can relax about the rivalry over Buddy; Joan is not a serious threat. The text bears point out this when Plath discloses that the reason for Buddy's visit is to invite Esther to Yale. Second, Joan is even more different than Esther is. Esther is bright and studious, poor and determined, pretty and well schooled in dating behavior. Joan is visibly ambitious (a quality women in the 1950s were trained to hide), but her real problem is the lack of physical beauty expected of women. Worse, she seems not to care about her appearance. Her later turn to lesbianism, then, seems a partial answer for her life.

Joan chooses to excel. She chooses to ask Buddy to Smith (because, the reader discovers later, of her admiration for his mother). More important, she chooses to become mad and be placed in the same sanatorium as Esther. Plath's assumption is that Joan later chooses her lesbian relationship and—whether or not directly related—her death. Again, Plath structures scenes so that their implications are more weighty than their actual intent. When Joan makes her first real appearance in *The Bell Jar*, at the sanatorium, the reader is quickly alerted to what Plath has already built into the text: "The big, horsey girl in jodhpurs sitting by the window glanced up with a broad smile" (159). The conversation between the women makes clear that Joan has been following Esther's psychological odyssey: "I've got a pile of clippings somewhere" (162). Joan's gift to Esther is the sequenced clippings, and although Esther is somewhat overwhelmed, she takes them and continues to wonder what her breakdown has had to do with Joan's. Joan's explanation is a quasi-comic non sequitur: "I read about you. . . . Not how they found you, but everything up to that, and I put all my money together and took the first plane to New York. . . . I thought it would be easier to kill myself in New York" (163).

Plath's attribution of Joan's attempted suicide to Esther is a sinister turn in the narrative, one based partly on her using Salinger's *The Catcher in the Rye* as model. By the end of that work, Holden Caulfield has faced incidents of both homosexuality and a friend's suicide; here Joan becomes the figure that will provide both for Esther. Careful to distance Esther from Joan, Plath gives the reader explicit instructions for understanding that Joan is not Esther, that Joan is someone Esther has always managed to keep a "cool distance" from. Esther says:

> I looked at Joan. In spite of the creepy feeling, and in spite of my old, ingrained dislike, Joan fascinated me. It was like observing a Martian, or a particularly warty toad. Her thoughts were not my thoughts, nor her feelings my feelings, but we were close enough so that her thoughts and feelings seemed a wry, black image of my own.
>
> Sometimes I wondered if I had made Joan up. Other times I wondered if she would continue to pop in at every crisis of my life to remind me of what I had been, and what I had been through, and carry out her own separate but similar crisis under my nose. (179)

The competition Esther feels for Joan's "progress" as she moves through the sanatorium, her envy at Joan's "success," carries the reader back to the initial competitive standing as the women show their interest in Buddy Willard. In the later section of the novel, Plath is careful to make Buddy more an object of ridicule for the two of them than an object of desire. As Joan says bluntly, "I never really liked Buddy Willard. He thought he knew everything. He thought he knew everything about women" (179).

Changing the focus of the women's competition from Willard to their mental health, Plath clears the way for Joan to explore her lesbianism. In her relationship with DeeDee, a situation Esther stumbles on accidentally, Joan brings to mind all the gossip about women couples at school, gossip Plath takes care to show is based on complete ignorance. As antidote to the sensationalized elements of lesbianism, the scene in which Esther defensively talks with Dr. Nolan about what women see in other women is entirely positive: "Tenderness" is Nolan's answer. In a novel, and world, in which so few examples of that quality exist, the word has great impact.

Joan's suicide, following what has appeared to be her near recovery, stuns the reader. The intervening episode has been Esther's going to Joan with the frightening bleeding after sexual intercourse, giving Joan the problem of saving her life while dealing with the injuries heterosexual penetration could inflict. Esther's extensive bleeding is imaged unforgettably in the stream of blood from her upheld shoe onto Joan's carpet. As Joan plays the good nurse, wrapping Esther in towel after towel, Plath leaves the reader to guess at the trauma Esther's wounding has inflicted on Joan: "she peeled back my blood-wet clothes, drew a quick breath as she arrived at the original royal red towel, and applied a fresh bandage. I lay, trying to slow the beating of my heart, as every beat pushed forth another gush of blood" (189). Joan's experience of calling doctors, only to be hung up on because it is a Sunday, is equally chilling. Rather than being a copy of Esther, Joan now finds herself an original, the friend responsible for Esther's very life. Again, the theme of choice as luxury surfaces: even though both women have attempted suicide, neither wants death to result from Esther's vaginal tear.

The juxtaposition of Joan's suicide by hanging with the hospital emergency room scene (in which the doctor on call assures Esther that the tear can be easily fixed, and that she is "one in a million" to have this wound) suggests a cause-and-effect relationship. What Plath provides in the text, however, discounts the "reasonable" interpretation. Esther talks with Dr. Nolan about Joan's death and states that she feels responsible for it. The scene in its entirety is as follows: " 'Of course you didn't do it!' I heard Doctor Nolan say. I had come to her about Joan, and it was the only time I remember her sounding angry. 'Nobody did it. *She* did it.' And then Doctor Nolan told me how the best of psychiatrists have suicides among their patients, and how they, if anybody, should be held responsible, but how they, on the contrary, do not hold themselves responsible" (196).

The structure of the novel does not allow the reader to take this comfort seriously, however. The last two scenes in the montage that *The Bell Jar* is inextricably link Joan's death with Esther's life through rebirth. As Esther attends Joan's funeral, sitting among the sorrowing mourners—most of them women—she thinks very little about Joan. Her thoughts are of herself, and her life and promise:

> [A]ll during the simple funeral service I wondered what I thought I was burying. . . . I took a deep breath and listened to the old brag of my heart.
>   I am, I am, I am. (198–99)

Following this scene and serving to conclude the novel is the capsule of the doctors' weekly board meeting and Esther's appearance at it. Dr. Nolan is sure Esther will be released, but Esther's confidence is even shakier than it would have been earlier. Through analysis, she has learned how difficult life—with all its encumbering decisions—can be: "I had hoped, at my departure, I would feel sure and knowledgeable about everything that lay ahead—after all, I had been 'analyzed.' Instead, all I could see were question marks" (199). But the triumphant ending of the book describes rebirth, Esther's following the "magical thread" of the physicians' eyes on her, as she leaves the institution for the real world once more.

Shadowed both in theme and in structure by Joan's death, Esther's leaving the protective care of the place and the physician/psychiatrist who has become her mentor, her shelter, is less than positive. Her earlier worry about the bell jar's descending appears again in the reader's mind; the death of one apparently "normal" and "successful" college woman undermines whatever optimism might be found in Esther's "recovery." To re-cover is itself ambiguous: to improve, or to cover again the sources of the original dilemma. And Esther's idiosyncratic description of herself as a retreaded tire, patched and imperfect, fits into this context.

The primary reason readers have difficulty finding *The Bell Jar* a satisfyingly "happy ending" novel is that Joan and Esther are forced to be partners during the last "recovery" segment of the text. While Plath was conscious of the differences between Joan and Esther, for most readers their similarities are also apparent—and the ease of considering Joan to be Esther's "double" more obviously achieved because of those similarities. They are each talented and academically gifted women, sharing a prestigious women's college education. They see themselves as separate from most of the other women at Smith. Even in her illness, Joan decides to become a psychiatrist (women in the 1950s were often discouraged from going to medical school or graduate school). They share the ambition to become professionals, to work once they have finished their education. They share a defiance of social norms for women—Joan in her lesbianism; Esther, in her readiness to have sexual experience before marriage. They don't let somewhat unorthodox physical appearances harm their social positions, and they seem to have enough of a sense of humor to comprehend how they differ from their friends—and to take pleasure in their differences, to a point.

Finally, however, the character of Joan Gilling becomes one of Plath's narrative ploys to reinforce Esther's coming to health. Even when both women are institutionalized, Esther's bewilderment at being an attempted suicide, subject to electroconvulsive shock treatments, and recuperating in the sanatorium varies greatly from Joan's almost-avaricious hunger for this new experience. Again, the reader is forced to realize how fully in control of her life economically Joan is, and the eventual irony of Joan's choosing to kill herself makes a statement that is as much economic as it is gender-based. Plath's use of Joan as a character shows that *The Bell Jar* is not about all women of the 1950s; rather it is about Esther Greenwood, a woman whose economic and social circumstances are much more restricted than those of her friends or acquaintances, who have more inherent power than she but may not make such good judgments or choices as they try to use that power to survive the inimical 1950s.

10

Esther Greenwood and Bell Jars

Plath's narrative of what happens to Esther Greenwood subtly underscores the dilemma of the choices Esther must make. By placing her protagonist in New York, surrounding her with lush fashion items and extravagant foods, the author suggests that this naive college woman is living hedonistically, experiencing life to the full. The setting is largely ironic, however, for Esther is so filled with guilt and insecurity that she cannot enjoy the freedom that might be hers. Her incipient worry clouds all the *Mademoiselle* activities, and when Jay Cee tries to talk seriously with her about her future, Esther panics and cannot remember what her ambitions are.

Living in New York serves to repress rather than free Esther. Identifying herself with women who wear sophisticated clothes, drink vodka, walk around the city at night, and have lovers, Esther instead finds herself uncomfortable, drunk and sick, frightened, and attacked by Marco. Before she leaves the city to return home, she throws her expensive clothes away from the top of the Amazon Hotel, an act that signifies her disillusionment as well as her despair.

The contrast between the crowded days of organized activity in New York and the dull days living at home, sleeping next to her mother, seeing only people who know Esther Greenwood as she was years earlier, works more to make the reader see how ill Esther has become than to glamorize the weeks she has spent in New York, for each scene in that initial, New York–based segment of the novel conveys the pervasive mood of Esther's worry. No matter what she accomplishes, it is not enough. No matter what she thinks she wants, when she achieves or acquires it, it is not enough. The enigmatic scene of Esther's being photographed with the rose, to signify her desire to be a poet, stands as the image of her frustration. When she sobs during the photo session, so hard that everyone in the room leaves her alone, the reader is left to confront Esther's pain as she expresses it—even if that pain seems inexplicable.

Plath's narrative structure emphasizes the nonrational "events" of Esther's life as it skips from one scene to another, fragmenting any coherence a novel might try to achieve. When a psyche disintegrates, reason has no role in its metamorphosis. A linear and apparently rational order, an explanation even hypothesized, is not appropriate. Only Mrs. Greenwood would expect order during a breakdown.

The shape of *The Bell Jar* exists to provide the reader with a means of experiencing that disintegration along with Esther. Keeping track of events, conjecturing causation, promulgating reasons—these are the tasks *The Bell Jar* mandates from a reader. Why, one might ask, does Esther leave Doreen outside in the hallway after she returns to the Amazon, drunk, on the night she meets Lenny Shepherd? Why does Esther agree to go with Marco, and then—when she has been assaulted—why does she keep his behavior secret, in effect helping him continue his abuse? Why does she leave the bloody streaks on her face but give her mother no other clues that she is distressed and disoriented? What is the meaning of all the symbology Esther creates to represent her life, instead of talking directly about what has happened to her?

Plath tries to help the reader gain viable insights by using a code of names, images, and ironies. The enigmas of *The Bell Jar* are often the means to its clearest expressions. The primary impression the reader is to have about Esther Greenwood, as Plath presents her, is that present-day Esther has little identity. She is confused, and whether her name is Elly or Elaine or Esther, she remains a disturbed—and distorted—young woman. In the opening scenes, Plath provides no conclusive answer for Esther's quandary about Doreen and Betsy: is Esther sexual and defiant like Doreen, or is she law-abiding and kind like Betsy? That both women seek Esther out and want to befriend her suggests that she appears to be like both. Rather than making Esther's complexity a positive trait, however, Plath leaves this aspect open to the reader's interpretation. Esther's complexity comes to represent her "problem." If she cannot fit into her culture in an identifiable way, even if that means she is limited to stereotypes, Esther has failed—and that failure is her fault.

The author purposely gives the reader this confused Esther so that the story of her breakdown and recovery builds dramatically to some kind of responsible clarity on Esther's part. The flashbacks to Esther's earlier history are carefully screened through the character's present-day confusion. The reader, then, is asked to create what a more objective telling of the experiences might be, to supply other segments of those experiences so that Esther's depressed versions of these happenings do not stand as entire, whole. They are obviously and necessarily partial. And because Esther cannot find anything good in her life to praise, she gives each reader a dour look at her past life. The rose-colored glasses of narrative observation in *The Bell Jar* have become blinders, and Esther cannot find anything that brings her happiness.

Plath's text shows clearly, however, that the reader does not need to accept Esther's view of her experience. Elsewhere in the novel, Plath provides some glimpses into Esther as she once was, Esther as her friends visualize and know her, Esther as her mother views her. As in real life, no person is a single facet; the narrative of Plath's novel allows the reader time and space to comprehend Esther from a variety of perspectives. This fairly conventional narrative tactic is itself undercut by irony, however. In the opening of the novel, for example, the reader assumes that the women living together in the Amazon Hotel will have a kind of camaraderie, that their microcosm of community will provide support particularly for the fragile Esther. What Plath shows, however, is that divisiveness and distance characterize these relationships, and the focal point—dissension over the Rosenberg execution—occurs within the women's community when Hilda, wearing a fashionable bile green hat, sets up the refrain, "I'm so glad they're going to die."

Plath's narrative strategy calls attention to Esther's disbelief when she hears what Hilda is really saying. She had anticipated the same shock and grief she herself knew at the executions of the couple. Plath gives readers some sense that Hilda will join with Esther's lament, as the women eat together in the hotel cafeteria. As Esther reflects,

> [A]t last I felt I had touched a human string in the cat's cradle of her heart. It was only as the two of us waited for the others . . . that Hilda amplified that Yes of hers.
> "It's awful such people should be alive." (82)

That damning statement is followed by Hilda's earlier comment, which so horrifies Esther and is used (three times) as a refrain: "I'm so glad they're going to die" (82).

Plath's thrice-repeated denial of humanity suggests that most famous denial in Western civilization, Peter's denial of Jesus. By changing the actual number of *Mademoiselle* College Board members—20—to the 12 of the novel, she further builds a religious structure. Esther Greenwood, despite her biblical-sounding name, would seldom be mistaken for a female Christ (at least to readers of the 1950s, trained almost exclusively in literature written by men about men)—but she could fit that martyred paradigm. Angry as Plath was about her education being so thoroughly male oriented, by the time of writing her novel (1961) she would have enjoyed such an intertextual joke. Read as a religious parody, *The Bell Jar* does have its saintly figures, its betrayers (Doreen as Judas), its Last Supper, its physical attack in the garden, and its burial away from civilization. Leaving the family members also takes on a different significance, as does Esther's "rebirth" at the end of the work.

The novel suggests that many of its events occur in disguise. Not only do people have trouble interpreting Esther as a character, literally reading her, but they have trouble naming her. Early in the text she abandons her weighty and positive name, "Esther," with its suggestions of bravery and sacrifice for a community, to become the frivolous "Elly Higginbottom" from Chicago rather than Boston. Defensively comic, Esther's lie occurs only after Lenny Shepherd (whose exploits make him a traditional "wolf" rather than anything associated with sheep) has made introducing "Doreen" into a sexual act, complete with touch ("Lenny slid his hand around Doreen's bare arm and gave her a squeeze"; 9). Whereas Doreen has recognized Lenny as someone famous because of his name, she readily adopts Elly as Esther's name—almost to the exclusion of remembering her friend's real name. Even though Esther is at first impressed that Doreen has caught the name and used it so quickly, she later wonders whether Doreen knows it is false. The counterpoint at Esther's hotel door—"Elly, Elly, Elly, let me in," juxtaposed with the maid's "Miss Greenwood, Miss Greenwood, Miss Greenwood"—leaves Esther confused, and she mentions that she feels as if she has "a split personality or something" (17). Anger at Doreen's easy assumption of her other identity may have led to Esther's leaving the woman in the hall, lying in her own vomit.

More obviously, when Esther begins her novel (the one that is to "fix" a lot of people), she names her protagonist Elaine and notes the similarity it has to Esther. Each name has six letters, each begins with an *E*, and each has some mythical significance. The Fair Elaine, the Lily Maid of Astolat, was a beauty who needed rescuing. When Esther rereads what she has written, she thinks of her character as "the barefoot doll in her mother's old yellow nightgown," sitting and staring into space. To be a doll is to assume an inanimate being, or the sexual familiarity of being a possession: a liberated and intellectual college woman would probably not want that identity. Choosing this language, wearing her mother's clothes, eating raw hamburger with egg in it, and planning alternatives to returning to college (apprenticing herself to a pottery maker, working her way to Germany and being a waitress, going to Europe and taking a lover)—Plath is plainly signaling the reader that Esther's reason is lost in her anxiety. She is making poor decisions, when she can make any at all: most of the time she sits and stares ahead, as if she had malaria. She knows how "scatty" her thinking is and chooses that word to describe the alternatives she has created.

Esther keeps the name Elly Higginbottom when she goes to Boston, dressed in what has become her customary disguise, Betsy's white blouse and green dirndl skirt. Walking through Boston Common with the sailor whose name she never learns, Esther creates a new identity to go along with her clothing and name: "I would be simple Elly Higginbottom, the orphan. People would love me for my sweet, quiet nature. They wouldn't be after me to read books and write long papers on the twins in James Joyce. And one day I might just marry a virile, but tender, garage mechanic and have a big cowy family, like Dodo Conway" (108).

The unknown sailor in this scene is expressly that—tender. He cares when Elly cries, mourns her being an orphan, and gives her the only support the reader has seen in the novel. Ironically, the sailor has no name, no money (he is in the service hoping to go to college someday on the GI bill), no history, and no promise. But Plath follows the Boston Common scene with Esther's second interview with the psychiatrist Dr. Gordon. Even though he remembers her proper name, it is clear that he is listening much less well than the young sailor does: he gives her pat answers, refuses to talk with her seriously, and sends her out so that he can speak with her mother about Esther's electroconvulsive shock treatments.

Plath structures this part of *The Bell Jar* so that there are two conclusions to this scene with Dr. Gordon. First is Esther's devastating experience when Gordon himself administers the shock treatment, causing Esther such pain and horror that she thinks to herself, "I wondered what terrible thing it was that I had done" (118). Punitive, relentless, Gordon's "treatments" will eventually damage Esther's sense of self so greatly that she will see suicide as the only alternative to this fearsome humiliation. When the doctor appears to talk with her as she is recuperating, her answers start him on his stories of World War II, as if he were caught in some repetitive fantasy. Second is Mrs.

Greenwood's admonishing Esther to get better so that the treatments can end. When Esther is able to speak of her hatred of Gordon—an important step in her coming to know her actual emotions—Mrs. Greenwood mishears what her daughter is saying, so as to cajole her to "get better": "I knew my baby wasn't like that. . . . I knew you'd decide to be all right again" (119). Esther has no recourse but to realize how alone she is. Neither her psychiatrist nor her mother understands—or even listens to—what she says.

Instead, Plath creates a montage of voices for *Esther* to listen to— the inarticulate man who gives her directions to Deer Island, the guard who calls her "Hey you," the men who call her "honey," and the bevy of assorted critical voices from memory that bombard her consciousness at will: "Doesn't your work interest you, Esther?"; "You know, Esther, you've got the perfect setup of a true neurotic"; and "You'll never get anywhere like that, you'll never get anywhere like that, you'll never get anywhere like that" (120). The final question for Esther in her prison house of language—misnamed, misaddressed, misheard, and misidentified—is, What does language mean? What does language do? Why do the incomprehensible words in James Joyce's *Ulysses* strike on her eyes and mind with no meaning whatsoever? Why can she not read? Why can she not write?

After Esther's suicide attempt and rescue, language misuse and misidentification continue. There is no difference between her state during the depths of her depression and her state after she is "recovering." The contortions of sight (she cannot see at all for a while), hearing, language, and then physical appearance (particularly as she gains weight because of the insulin shock treatments) continue Esther's anxiety: nothing is as it should be; nothing is recognizable. And the apparent malaise that confronting her world creates in Esther forces her into a catatonic still point. Eventually, after the insulin shock breakthrough, Esther begins to see and hear once again. Dr. Nolan can affect her: Esther can hear her voice. And it is as if Esther is relearning not only her world but rules about her world. She has been freed from her hoard of erroneous knowledge and is able to learn new and more useful skills for living. Plath is careful to emphasize that

Esther cannot simply forget the past: everything that has happened to her has had great meaning, and she has learned from all those experiences, no matter how unpleasant. Knowledge is never abstract, and the person grows from the daily trials of experience. Thus, Esther can face Buddy Willard with equanimity, and some sympathy. She can feel sorrow over Joan's suicide. She can feel apprehension over her interview with the board of physicians.

Freed to feel that emotion, of whatever kind, Esther can look at Buddy Willard when he comes to visit and feel, "Nothing. Nothing but a great, amiable boredom" (194). She can correct his assumption that there is something still "wrong" with her. But the scene exists at least partly so that Esther can look out across the snowy expanse of fields and recognize the newness—of terrain and of life—before her: "The sun, emerged from its gray shrouds of clouds, shone with a summer brilliance on the untouched slopes. Pausing in my work to overlook that pristine expanse, I felt the same profound thrill it gives me to see trees and grassland waist-high under flood water—as if the usual order of the world had shifted slightly, and entered a new phase" (195).

For all the brevity of the closing four episodes in *The Bell Jar*, Plath makes clear that Esther has indeed entered a "new phase." She asks Irwin to take care of the emergency room bill and, as a result, "[feels] perfectly free" (198). She attends Joan's funeral not only with sorrow but with the affirmation of her own power of selfhood: "I am, I am, I am" (199). And she enters her new birth ritual, the process of leaving the asylum for the real world, with as much confidence as an intelligent person can muster. The command from her beloved Dr. Nolan is both a directive and a blessing. It is the simple three-word phrase "All right, Esther." The name is correct, the approval is correct, and the procedure is what Esther Greenwood has needed her entire life (and her entire story): acceptance to be herself, to live in a world of free choices, to escape from the coercive restrictions of the bell jar of social opinion. There is no question that Plath intended to create a thoroughly positive ending for Esther's narrative.

11

Sylvia Plath and Bell Jars

Plath would herself have recognized the frustration of having no language: she became a writer so that she would always be in control of expressing the truths she saw in life. When she creates Esther Greenwood's ultimate frustration with Buddy Willard, it is over his control of words, not his control of their emotional relationship. As Esther thinks to herself, "I spent a lot of time having imaginary conversations with Buddy Willard. He was a couple of years older than I was and very scientific, so he could always prove things. When I was with him I had to work to keep my head above water."

In the context of Esther's later suicide attempt by drowning, this image of keeping her head above water seems as sinister as it sounds. She feels powerless: Buddy is older, better (or at least differently) educated, and intent on taking their conversations into areas of his expertise. Esther continues, "These conversations I had in my mind usually repeated the beginnings of conversations I'd really had with Buddy, only they finished with me answering him back quite sharply, instead of just sitting around and saying 'I guess so' " (46). While there are many comic scenes in the novel built on this structure, with the reader cheering Esther on for defiant and sharp-witted answers, the underlying power struggle remains unresolved. The ending of the novel focuses on Esther's rebirth as a person, beginning her life as language speaker anew, shaken out of the dialogue mode by the trauma of her breakdown.

Even though at the end of the novel the reader is not interested in Esther's dating situation (or is less interested in it than in her saving—and finding—her life), the bell jar consists partly of social pressure to marry. In the 1950s women could not dismiss considerations of mating even if they were liberated people who wanted to be in control of their own language. At the depths of Esther's depression, she counts her failures in terms of being a good wife: she cannot cook, she is a poor dancer, she is too tall, and so on. Much as in her late poem "The Applicant," Plath recognized all too well that many of her positive traits were detriments on the marriage market. In this respect, the autobiographical elements of the 1950s culture appeared without disguise in her first novel.

A more troubling theme, however—one Plath may not have realized would grow to the prominence it came to have—concerns the interference of Esther's mother in her life: the shaping of the daughter's psyche by the oversolicitous, overinvolved mother. It is this theme and its ramifications that led Plath to call *The Bell Jar* a "potboiler" and to warn her brother Warren not to tell their mother about the book.[31] Her decision to publish it in England under a pseudonym was one means of protecting her mother, and her mother's friends, from any hurt feelings. Even though as a writer, Plath knew that no fiction was ever autobiographical—or at least not simply autobiographical—she also knew that readers who were not writers themselves often made errors in attribution ("This character *is* this person").

Plath saw *The Bell Jar* as an account, in fictionalized manner, of the traumatic events of her life: the move inland to Wellesley after her father's death, her breakdown and suicide attempt, her experiences with Dick Norton and other repressive and macho boyfriends, and her month in New York on the *Mademoiselle* College Board in 1953. The student of many different writing teachers in both high school and college, Plath knew she needed events and action to make her narrative of interest, and she thought the comic tone—at least of the opening—would also make what she had to write about more palatable. She further had in mind using some of the techniques that two of her favorite writers, J. D. Salinger and Philip Roth, had been experimenting with. The novel that stayed closest to her during the writing of *The Bell Jar* was Salinger's *The Catcher in the Rye*, one of the first American novels to deal with an adolescent's breakdown. Holden Caulfield became a model for the honest, well spoken, and obviously sane protagonist who finds himself at odds with a culture and a family that are moving farther and farther away from sanity.

Esther Greenwood's story begins before the breakdown and ends with some resolution (Caulfield, at the ending of *Catcher*, is still in the midst of telling his story to a psychiatrist). Like Caulfield, Esther appreciates the ridiculousness of her plight. Her perceptions set her outside society but do not free her from the pressures of that world. Plath carefully sets the story of Esther in the context of a world political situation as well (not for nothing had she been reading Camus and Sartre), the controversial execution of the Rosenbergs. Esther Greenwood's personal horror at what she finds in life is set against the horror of the Rosenbergs' executions by electric shock.

Plath's choice of her grandmother's maiden name, Greenwood, was satisfying for reasons both symbolic and personal, and because the novel moves toward Esther's rebirth, the image of green wood is comforting. In *The Bell Jar*, Esther is a survivor: she maintains a sense of humor, a cool if cynical view of life that colors the grim comedy of her descriptions. She is also—at the time she records her story—a mother, a practical woman who has made the best of her life and who continues to try to learn from it. Like Caulfield or Elizabeth in Shirley Jackson's *The Bird's Nest*, Esther Greenwood is not ashamed of her descent into madness. She wants to tell about it, partly to rid herself of memories (or to shape those memories so as to have control of them) and partly to help other women faced with the same kind of social and family pressure.

Writing *The Bell Jar* was a liberating experience for Plath. Frieda had been born the year before, and Sylvia, having recovered from an appendectomy and a miscarriage less than a year after the child's birth, was finally strong enough to enjoy writing at some length. Trading off child care with Ted, she went each morning to the Merwins' flat (which had been offered to Ted for his work while the Merwins were on vacation) and wrote for three or four hours. For the first time in her professional life, the writing provided continuity for Sylvia. The long prose work had its own rhythms. It was easier to return to it each morning than it would have been to begin a new poem, or a short story. As she would later recall, she could use everything in a novel: the writer's life was fair game, including all experiences and emotional nuances. For example, Plath borrowed a sexual experience that occurred on a blind date she had gone on during her freshman year at Smith, and in the novel attributed it to Buddy Willard.

Keeping the narrative of the novel going, when in fact many of the events were not in any way real, or at least had not occurred in the time sequence of the novel or with the people included, was Plath's biggest problem. To solve some of the narrative difficulties, she relied on Salinger's *The Catcher in the Rye*. For instance, Holden meets a sailor and a Cuban; so does Esther. Holden walks 41 blocks back to his New York hotel; Esther walks 48. Holden looks as yellow in his mirror as Esther (looking Chinese) does in hers. He vomits before he goes to bed, as Doreen does early in *The Bell Jar*. Later, Esther and the 11 other editors are extremely ill from ptomaine poisoning—and so there is ample opportunity for vomiting scenes.

Both novels have a moving cemetery scene. *Catcher* has its violent and bloody suicide in James Castle's death, which in *The Bell Jar* becomes the suicide by hanging. (Joan's death is also modeled fictionally on the death of a freshman student at Smith the year Plath was teaching English there. The issue of the campus paper, the *Sophian*, that published an interview with Plath also included the somber story of the woman who hanged herself beside the scenic Paradise Pond.)[32]

Holden wants to go to the West because he thinks that wilder part of the country will save his psyche; Esther wants to go to Chicago, and lies about being from that city, for the same reason. The suggestion of Esther's discovering Joan's lesbianism parallels Holden's discovery of the homosexuality of Mr. Antolini, his friend and former teacher. That discovery precipitates Holden's breakdown. For Esther, the suspicion of Joan's sexual preference is less important than the fact of her death, but Joan's witnessing Esther's bleeding after intercourse may have led to her suicide. Unraveling the sexual texts is necessary in both novels, and uncommon in fiction of the 1950s.

In both novels, readers care what happens to the protagonist partly because the narrative is conveyed in the character's voice. Much of the comedy of each text grows from the idiosyncratic expressions of Holden and Esther, and for many students today, little "literature" has ever seemed quite so fresh, so much a replication of the voices that surround them daily. With the quick shifts in mood and tone that the voice engaged in storying can achieve, both novels keep the reader's attention by moving rapidly from scene to scene, mood to mood. This is true of the opening of *The Bell Jar*.

Plath deviates from the model of Salinger's book in her intense need to have readers understand that Esther has recovered. *Catcher* ends in the midst of Holden's telling his story; Esther moves past retelling to the act of leaving the institution. She can therefore be seen as a woman who has come through both Dante's hell and her own, to find her fulfillment not in some idealized Beatrice, the symbolic unattainable woman/spirit, but in herself as flesh-and-blood person.

Part of Plath's insistence on being able to create a genuine woman character who is more real than idealized, and to shape a fiction from reality, grew from her belief that women writers were neglected in all literary study. As Sandra Gilbert and others have proved, Plath's interest during 1961 and 1962 was focused intently on Virginia Woolf, Stevie Smith, Eudora Welty, and other women writers—not to mention Anne Sexton, Adrienne Rich, and other women poets contemporary with her.[33] To write fiction about women, Plath was searching both within and without: testing what she knew to be true about women's themes and women's involvement in the creative process against what other women writers had said about those matters over time.

One of the difficulties Plath and her contemporaries found in writing fiction about women characters was that unless the shape of the narrative differed radically from standard genres, women would be cast in secondary roles: playing wife, daughter, lover, sister, or mother to the primary protagonist, who was more than likely male. Plath's narrative focused on the 12 women in New York, moving then to a single woman who lived at home and finally to an institution filled with women, a design that helped her avoid the usual problem of having to subordinate women characters to men characters. Plath in fact chose to emphasize the segments of Esther's narrative precisely so that the femaleness of the work came through clearly.

Imaginatively, throughout the novel the reader is nearly as conscious of Esther's mother as of Buddy Willard: in Esther's life, for all her attention to finding a suitable man and marrying, her immediate and significant conflicts occur with Mrs. Greenwood. The relationship between the self-sacrificing mother, who says her daughter's well-being is the most important consideration in her life, and the daughter, who both admires and resents her mother's example and control, lies at the heart of *The Bell Jar*. As a corollary to the mother-daughter bond itself is the question of motherhood. Does a woman's sense of self and the full understanding of her sexuality depend on her giving birth, as some psychologists of the 1950s theorized? Is the lockstep pattern of women's lives—education, marriage, motherhood—dominant for healthy psychological reasons?

For all its many plot elements, *The Bell Jar* seems to be focused on these questions as its core. Such characters as Dodo Conway, Philomena Guinea (her very name suggesting the violent punishment the angry male creates, robbing her of language forever), the old poet at Esther's college, and Jay Cee are described in terms of their being mothers or choosing not to be mothers. Only heterosexual relationships are viable because having children is the desired outcome; sex for pleasure is suspicious if not immoral. Plath builds the matriarchal patterns and questions into the text through imagery and language, as well as episode. In the scene of Esther's observing Dodo Conway from her bedroom window, for example, Dodo is depersonalized through her pregnancy: "A woman not five feet tall, with a grotesque, protruding stomach, was wheeling an old black baby carriage down the street. Two or three small children of various sizes, all pale, with smudgy faces and bare smudgy knees, wobbled along in the shadow of her skirts. A serene, almost religious smile lit up the woman's face. Her head tilted happily back, like a sparrow egg perched on a duck egg, she smiled into the sun" (95). These are not healthy children. They are shrouded in their mother's skirt, while she seems to gain her happiness from her belief in the sanctity of being pregnant (through hardly human in the process). Plath describes the Conway house as "morbid," showing the children's nutrition as sadly deficient—yet despite real weaknesses as a mother, Dodo is beloved by the neighborhood.

In contrast, Esther shrinks from the sight of Dodo and her brood, crawling back into bed, hiding from the woman's sight, and stating to herself, "Children made me sick." The images of virginity and purity that follow, in the scene in which Esther attempts to write a novel— that is, to give birth in her own way, to her own product—create a subtext for the theme that motherhood is both expected and desirable. This passage in *The Bell Jar* concludes with the scene of Esther's observing her mother asleep in the twin bed beside her, a scene that seems cruel if removed from the context of the dilemma of motherhood as life role. The racing mind of Esther, caught in another sleepless night, jumps from alternative to alternative: "I saw the years of my life spaced along a road in the form of telephone poles, threaded together by wires. I counted one, two, three . . . nineteen telephone poles, and then the wires dangled into space, and try as I would, I couldn't see a single pole beyond the nineteenth" (101). The image suggests the inevitability of the woman's life choices—yet tantalizing with incompletion. If Esther does not marry and have children, does not become Dodo Conway, then what will be her alternatives?

Plath juxtaposes that acutely imaged meditation with the view of Esther's mother: "My mother turned from a foggy log into a slumbering middle-aged woman, her mouth slightly open and a snore raveling from her throat." Just as Dodo was dehumanized by her pregnancy, Esther's mother moves between the dehumanization of "log" and the snoring middle-aged woman, depending on Esther's own level of perception. Annoyed by the sound of the snores and frustrated by her own sleeplessness (and even more by the indecision of her future), Esther hypothesizes her mother's death: "The piggish noise irritated me, and for a while it seemed to me that the only way to stop it would be to take the column of skin and sinew from which it rose and twist it to silence between my hands" (101). In the need to rid herself of the frustration of meaningless sound, Esther briefly thinks of killing her mother, the source of the unpleasant sound. Again, her dehumanized description helps to hide the evil of her thoughts from herself—"piggish" noise, "column of skin and sinew" rather than throat. Finally, however, as the next paragraph shows, Esther is overcome by her guilt: she wants "more weight," as she crawls beneath her mattress, hoping to be crushed. Many of her suicide attempts that follow involve returning to a catatonic or womblike state. And her final attempt leaves her hidden in a pocket of stony dirt under the family house, as if she were a fetus of the structure in fact as well as in metaphor.

Esther's desire to be an orphan, to escape the maternal presence by denying it; her envisioning the strange brown-clothed woman on the Boston Common as her mother, *a* mother; and her continued reversion in imagination to the sight of the malformed fetuses during Buddy's hospital tour—all these things suggest both a great aversion to and a great fear of motherhood. Her feeling of real triumph when Dr. Nolan makes it possible for her to be fit with a diaphragm—and thereby escape any pregnancy that casual sex might cause—speaks to her need to separate sexuality from the more complex burden of motherhood, a much larger dilemma and choice than she is ready for at 19.

As Nancy Chodorow and Marilyn Yalom have said repeatedly, motherhood is a socially constructed reality and, because of same-sex bonding, daughters are both more critical and more appreciative of their mothers. They identify with the female parent so strongly that coming to be a separate self is often difficult, and their innate dependence on the mother causes anxiety. Add to this (a) the necessary anxiety any woman feels about giving birth and (b) the obvious complications the creative woman can predict with children in the household and Plath's reasons for writing a novel so fixated on the quandary of motherhood are not difficult to decipher. As Yalom writes, "Women are . . . faced with a uniquely frightening ordeal in the form of childbirth. Because it is so common and because its casualties are often difficult to assess, we tend to underestimate the impact of childbirth upon the mother's mental health. . . . [C]hildbirth constitutes an alarming episode in their lives and a key factor in their mental illnesses. . . . The female body as proving ground for the adult woman is one of the central themes" (Yalom, 4–5, 7).[34]

Underlying these fearful thoughts of motherhood are the more pervasive worries of mortality, worries Plath would have understood on losing her father while she was a child. Esther's search for her father's grave and her sorrowful mourning for him are a parallel to her more fearful quest to investigate the sexuality that leads to pregnancy and birth—and motherhood. The fear of one's own death, as posited by Rollo May and Ernest Becker, philosophers Plath read, is primary, and learned early when a parent dies. As Yalom summarizes,

> *The Bell Jar* is constructed upon the bedrock of significant existential experiences: the protracted illness and early death of the author/heroine's father that filled her with lifelong anxiety; the rite of passage into adulthood necessitating choice and forcing a discovery of her own aging process; and the escape into madness as a reaction to intolerable internal and external stress. But it also bears witness to female specificity, most notably in the recurrent images of decaying figs, dead babies, jarred foetuses, and other forms of aborted maternity that are objective correlatives of the protagonist's inner state of terror. . . . Paradoxically, one way of denying the absolute reality of death is by taking control of it—by killing yourself before death kills you. (Yalom, 14)

The meticulous control Esther takes of the process of her suicide, her diffidence toward relinquishing any power as she might ask for help, and her disappointment when she wakes to find she is alive and reasonably whole support Yalom's reading of motivation here.

For Anthony Libby, too, Plath's attempted suicide as charted in

The Bell Jar becomes part of a larger philosophical stance, the solution to what Libby describes as the more general poetic preoccupation at midcentury with "negation, darkness, and death." Libby sees much of American literature influenced by Becker (and Heidegger), and Plath as particularly susceptible to the need for the experience of the *via negativa*. Poets of what Libby calls "immanence" force their psychic lives downward, always searching for transcendence but willing to travel "into the unconscious as well as into the flow of physical being through death."[35] Free of gender considerations, Plath's search—and her work—compares with that of Robert Bly, Theodore Roethke, Robert Lowell, Anne Sexton, and W. S. Merwin.

While one must recognize that Plath was a part of the mixed currents of the 1950s culture, arguments that place her in a particularly female world seem undeniable. Both in *The Bell Jar* and in her aesthetic statements, as well as throughout her poems, Plath defines her life experience and her work as feminine. Indeed, part of her success during the 1960s was that she had begun to realize how to use the wealth of real experiences her life as woman had given her. She seemed content to leave off the imitating that had been responsible for some of the lifeless writings of her earlier years. It is no accident that in Plath's essay about being a novelist (written in 1962), she describes the novelist as a woman:

> I imagine her, then, pruning a rosebush with a large pair of shears, adjusting her spectacles, shuffling about among the teacups, humming, arranging ashtrays or babies, absorbing a slant of light, a fresh edge to the weather, and piercing, with a kind of modest, beautiful X-ray vision, the psychic interiors of her neighbors—her neighbors on trains, in the dentist's waiting room, in the corner teashop. To her, this fortunate one, what is there that *isn't* relevant? . . . Her business is Time, the way it shoots forward, shunts back, blooms, decays and double-exposes itself. Her business is people in Time.[36]

The humanization of the aesthetic process, here a brief year after Plath had drafted *The Bell Jar*, stands in warming contrast to the dehumanization she used to depict Mrs. Greenwood in her novel. For all the pressures and depression of her last year alive, Plath seems to have come to know the comfort of writing well. She was happy to be a woman novelist, and to lay claim to the light, weather, babies, and tasks that constituted women's lives.

12

Earlier Partial Versions of *The Bell Jar*

As Ted Hughes points out in his introduction to *Johnny Panic and the Bible of Dreams*—Plath's collection of stories, essays, and other prose fragments—the writer's "painful subjectivity was her real theme . . . the plunge into herself was her only real direction."[37] His assessment is as true of Plath's fiction as of her poetry. Much of the short fiction she wrote, from middle school until her death, was about a girl or woman protagonist caught in an emotional situation that had no quick or simple solution. The protagonist was usually set at variance with her culture and her social norms, and had few if any friends or supporters to help her reach decisions. Other girls or women were adversaries, not colleagues, and the characters were often in competition for a prize of either male attention or academic honor.

While many of Plath's stories are based in part on her own experience, she herself drew a careful, conscious line between autobiography and fiction. Late in 1962, in an interview with Peter Orr for the BBC, she explained, "I cannot sympathize with these cries from the heart that are informed by nothing except a needle or a knife or whatever it is. I believe that one should be able to control and manipulate experiences, even the most terrifying—like madness, being tortured, this kind of experience—and one should be able to manipulate these experiences with an informed and intelligent mind."[38] For Plath, the line between "autobiographical" writing, when the term is used pejoratively, and writing that expresses themes of deep importance to the writer has become blurred. Because many of the events she writes about in *The Bell Jar* are autobiographical (or partly based on events that did happen), readers have assumed that her fiction sprang from those same roots—even in the case of stories about fantasy or dream. Rather than using factually autobiographical materials, Plath appears to have used and reused images and themes to give insights into both her own view of herself and the problems and situations that troubled—or interested—her most.

Among the early stories housed in the Lilly Library Plath Archive at Indiana University, many are apparently based on the writer's experience. "Among the Bumblebees" describes in remarkable depth a young girl's feelings when her father dies; "Tongues of Stone" charts the woman protagonist's feelings while she recovers from severe depression; the Johnny Panic story describes the fantasy of a "dream recorder," a woman who works in the psychiatric ward of a city hospital (as Plath did at Massachusetts General Hospital in the late 1950s). What is more pervasive about this fiction than its sense of real experience is its emphasis on one of Plath's later dominant themes—that of the different woman, the woman (or girl) who feels she is different from society's expectations and perhaps from her own, and therefore feels excluded. In some stories the woman is a classic overachiever, but in others she enjoys walking her own path.

One of the earliest of Plath's unpublished stories is "The Dark River," dated 1949, when the author would have been 17. The protagonist, an older woman, tells her life story to a young woman listener. What is important about this rather Poe-like gothic story of the older woman's love affair is less her maneuver to free herself from her lover than her intense rapport with her young listener. The most vivid part of her story concerns the woman's escape from the man who loved her, an unusual thematic emphasis for the 1940s and 1950s, when most women married: "It was good to run. As her feet thudded over the gravel path, the blood pounded in her ears and drowned out the sound of the river, which still echoed in her brain. Something pent up inside her broke, free and wild. Her hair flew out behind her as she ran, and her eyes were blinded by the warm, compassionate rain."[39] Plath's high school writing covers the expected themes—young women characters who want to be writers, girls trying to be cool on dates, lonely older women who have chosen to live alone. Yet it also introduces other women who have made that choice and been reasonably successful. Her 1949 "East Wind," for example, introduces the character of a lonely professional woman, "Miss Minton," who follows an elfin child through city streets at nightfall, lured to a near suicide on a river bridge; some years later, the unmarried Minton sister becomes the heroine of Plath's prizewinning story "Sunday at the Mintons' " (1952), in which the woman's difference has become positive, humorous, and even superior to the demeanor of her more obviously successful brother.

The authoritative brother, Henry, gives directions, plans the family life, and is continually amazed at the trepidation of his shadowy and fragile sister Elizabeth. Plath's letters to her mother make clear that Henry was based in part on the character of Dick Norton (the Buddy Willard character of *The Bell Jar*) and that Elizabeth represented the author as she saw herself within the boundaries of the relationship with Norton. Worksheets for the story in the manuscript collection include Plath's lists of traits for each character. Henry's list included the terms *perseverence, firmness, stability, patient, indefatigable, solid, sturdy, staunch*, and the more negative *plodding, obstinate, dogmatic, relentless*, and *designing*. For Elizabeth, Plath's list reads *fluctuate, tremulous, capricious* (twice), *frothy, volatile, frail, erratic, fanciful, whimsical, spontaneous*, and the somewhat more critical *eccentric, freakish, giddy*, and *shudder*. What occurs in the story is a moderation of these qualities, with Henry's character becoming less objectionable—except in its relation to Elizabeth—and Elizabeth's becoming both stronger and more likeable.

Plath is able to create some memorable scenes that convey the characters' differences. The opening describes Elizabeth, who "leaned dreamily aslant his mahogany desk for a moment," dreaming of the sea and envisioning waves crashing along the shore, when Henry's voice calling her interrupts her reverie. Her new role of keeping house for her successful brother jars with the freedom she has known as a librarian, and much of the story shows her strategy to escape the almost-neurotic scrutiny of her careful brother. Plath's mature crafting of scenes that show Elizabeth's "vague, imprecise world" set against Henry's demands for order gives such comic dialogues as this:

"Last spring . . ."

"The week of April sixth," Henry prompted.

"Yes, of course. You know, I never thought," she said, "of what direction I was going in on the map . . . up, down or across."

Henry looked at his sister with something like dismay. "You never have!" he breathed incredulously. "You mean you never figure whether you're going north or south or east or west?"

"No," flashed Elizabeth, "I never do. I never saw the point."

She thought of his study, then, the walls hung with the great maps, carefully diagrammed, meticulously annotated. . . . She imagined herself wandering, small and diminutive, up the finely drawn contour lines and down again, wading through the shallow blue ovals of lakes. . . .

Henry was looking at her still with something akin to shock. She noted that his eyes were very cold and very blue. . . . Elizabeth could see him now, standing brightly in the morning on the flat surface of a map, watching expectantly for the sun to come up from the east. (He would know exactly where east was). . . . Feet planted firmly he stood with pencil and paper making calculations, checking to see that the world revolved on schedule.[40]

Part of the success of this narrative lies in Plath's being able to create humor, and her gentle handling of both characters, not only the one she understands best. The ending of the story, however, shows Elizabeth winning in a physical contest with Henry, and only her charity saves him from death. For Plath, the woman who knew her own mind and went her own way was continuously heroic.

Five years later, in "Stone Boy with Dolphin," Plath's mood is much more aggressive. The character of Dody Ventura is harshly outside—she is an American in England, a young woman writer in a culture that recognizes male artists. Tough and cynical ("As long as it was someone who didn't matter, it didn't matter," Dody thinks of her sexual intimacy with a date), she longs for something to draw her into life: "Let something happen. Something terrible, something bloody."[41] The title image of the story, the rococo statue in Dody's courtyard, needs to be shattered just as her own stoic calm needs to be jarred. In this story, the theme of artist-as-outsider carries a more sexual connotation. Woman is not only inferior intellectually and emotionally, according to her society, but she is also inferior physically: Dody becomes not only an outsider but a victim.

That "Stone Boy with Dolphin" is one of Plath's most elliptical stories may stem from the fact that in the late 1950s, very few people were writing explicitly about sexual experience. To be descriptive—except through the image of smashed statues—was a risk Plath was not yet ready to take. (That *The Bell Jar* has repeatedly been banned and taken out of secondary school libraries in the 1980s and 1990s suggests that Plath's approach to sexual topics was ahead of its time, and our own. Her deference to the established literary conventions, in what she could not write about sexual experience, suggests that she understood all too well what her role as a woman writer was to be.)

"Stone Boy with Dolphin" is an angry story, but its anger alternates with extreme passivity: the resultant portrait of the young American woman is fragmented and troubling. Plath will later draw her women characters more directly, although still in metaphor, and often depicting them in relation to a powerful male writer as the object of personal desire.

Several other of Plath's stories from the 1950s provide a more wistful picture of the poet-persona searching for a stable concept of justice and honor, a way to live that satisfies both her needs and those of conventional society. Both "Superman and Paula Brown's New Snowsuit" and "The Shadow" are stories about a girl who feels herself different from the rest of the neighborhood children. Whether she is ostracized from her friends because she is more adventurous or tougher, she is made to feel that being different is morally wrong.

Other stories use fantasy to show the feeling of isolation of the unusual or gifted person. "The Wishing Box" recounts the rivalry between newlyweds about the quality and quantity of their individual dreams. "Sweetie Pie and the Gutter Men" suggests the alliance between an ill-behaved child of Myra Wardle's college friend and Myra herself—an almost-demonic satisfaction with their "badness," an obvious kind of difference. "The Fifty-ninth Bear" sets a husband and wife in competition as they race to see bear no. 59. In each story, the woman protagonist is made to feel inferior for being outside the pale of social (male-dominated and male-constructed) convention.

It is difficult to find much of Plath's fiction that does not in some way deal with the theme of individual difference and a culture's fear of what it sees to be the unusual. Like most writers, Sylvia Plath chose to work toward expression of her deepest concerns, fears, and enthusiasms. And like most writers, she found her own psyche—with the aggression that gave her the strength to be a writer—to be of great interest to her. Like a shred of platinum, the artist's personality transforms experience and shapes it into art. What might Plath's short fiction have been had she not insisted on seeing herself as "a reject . . . old and lonely. As from a star I saw, coldly and soberly, the separateness of everything. I felt the wall of my skin: I am I. That stone is a stone"[42] As she had written in her journal in 1949, when she was 17, "I feel free—unbound by responsibility, I still can come up to my own private room, with my drawings hanging on the walls. . . . I am very happy. . . . I am afraid of getting older. I am afraid of getting married. Spare me from cooking three meals a day—spare me from the relentless cage of routine and rote. I want to be free—free to know people and their backgrounds—free to move to different parts of the world. . . . I want, I think, to be omniscient."[43]

The critic Melody Zajdel agrees that much of Plath's short fiction served as testing ground for The Bell Jar, and that Plath would not have written her novel so quickly and with such polish had she not already accomplished sections of it within her shorter fiction. Zajdel points to "Tongues of Stone," "Sweetie Pie and the Gutter Men," "Johnny Panic and the Bible of Dreams," and "In the Mountains" as the works that in some cases include "episodes with the same actions, characters, images, sometimes even the same words." The controversial section from the novel in which Esther lies sleepless beside her snoring mother and wishes her quiet—perhaps dead—occurs first in "Tongues of Stone," for the purpose of having Esther realize "there is neither parental security nor any meaningful reason to continue being in either the present or the future."[44] Wanting to smother under the mattress, attempting suicide by drug-taking and strangulation, experiencing the insulin treatment—Plath's story describes all these episodes that reappear in the novel.

"In the Mountains" is a more sympathetic account of Buddy Willard (here, Austin) at the tuberculosis sanatorium. Vulnerable and shaken by his illness, Austin needs the reassurance of Esther/Isobel, although his marriage proposal operates in the same way, to cast her as his possession through naming her entirely as wife. The "Sweetie Pie" story recounts a scene of childbirth that affects the protagonist in the same way Mrs. Tomolillo's giving birth does in the novel, and the "Johnny Panic" story includes the horrifying account of the electroconvulsive shock treatment, when Dr. Gordon fails to administer it properly and effectively.

Zajdel sees thematic parallels, too, in that Plath consistently fears the death of imagination, the problem of the writer (or a like figure) alienated and punished by the "real world" for the very qualities that should make the imaginative consciousness valuable. More important than the obvious reuse of material from the earlier stories is that they do prefigure *The Bell Jar* in their "continued thematic concern with two interrelated ideas: first, the idea of living and sustaining a life of the imagination, and second, the socio-mythic form of this theme, what Josephine Donovan has called 'the sexual politics of Sylvia Plath' " (Zajdel, 182).[45]

The Bell Jar was written to give Esther Greenwood primacy in the real world that categorized her as a woman who has had a breakdown and tried to commit suicide. Her institutionalization marks her as fragile, different, objectionable—and those months and experiences are part of her life forever. Faced with a culture hostile to the foreignness of this experience, a culture that wants to pretend that all people's lives are (or should be) the same, Esther Greenwood spends whatever energy and imagination she can muster to simply endure. Opposed by an unfeeling and ignorant society, represented by her mother's belief that not ever mentioning that breakdown year will somehow erase it from being, Esther fights hard for the right to be the survivor, rather than the victim, of her experiences. If the ending of the novel is less convincing than readers might desire, Plath was writing as truly as she could about the problems of rehabilitation and recovery in the midst of this judgmental and unsympathetic milieu. Any rebirth was an accomplishment. Any remission from Esther's feared bell jar was a victory.

Notes and References

1. Douglas Miller and Marion Nowak, *The Fifties: The Way We Really Were* (Garden City, N.Y.: Doubleday, 1977), 147–81.

2. *The Journals of Sylvia Plath*, ed. Frances McCullough (New York: Dial Press, 1982), 102, 107, 125, and 152. As Plath writes on p. 124, "I am still young. Even twenty-three and a half is not too late to live anew."

3. Aurelia Plath, introduction to *Letters Home by Sylvia Plath: Correspondence 1950–1963*, ed. Aurelia Schober Plath (New York: Harper & Row, 1975), 12–13.

4. Linda W. Wagner, "Plath's *Ladies' Home Journal* Syndrome," *Journal of American Culture* 7 (Spring–Summer 1984):32–38. For a thorough discussion of women's lives during the 1950s, see Eugenia Kaladin, *Mothers and More: American Women in the Fifties* (Boston: Twayne, 1984).

5. Catharine R. Stimpson, "Literature as Radical Statement," in *Columbia Literary History of the United States*, ed. Emory Elliott (New York: Columbia University Press, 1988), 1064, and Ellen Moers, *Literary Women* (Garden City, N.Y.: Doubleday, 1976), xv.

6. Charles Molesworth, "Culture, Power, and Society," in *Columbia Literary History*, ed. Elliott, 1031.

7. Marilyn Yalom, *Maternity, Mortality, and the Literature of Madness* (University Park: Pennsylvania State University Press, 1985), 2, 5; hereafter cited in text.

8. Jerome Mazzaro, "The Cycles of History: Sylvia Plath," in *Postmodern American Poetry* (Urbana: University of Illinois Press, 1980), 154.

9. Robert Taubman, "Anti-heroes," *New Statesman*, 25 January 1963, 127–28; Laurence Lerner, "New Novels," *Listener*, 31 January 1963, 215; Rupert Butler, "New American Fiction: Three Disappointing Novels—but One Good One," *Time and Tide*, 31 January 1963, 34. Other reviews listed in Sheryl Meyering's *Sylvia Plath: A Reference Guide, 1973–1988* are similarly positive: Anthony Burgess notes Plath's "sensitivity and decorum" rather than a sensational approach to the theme (*Observer*, 27 January 1963, 22); Ruby

Millar finds Plath displaying "a surety of aim and startling deftness of phrase" (*Derbyshire Times*, 15 February 1963, 17); and Faith Faulconbridge calls it an admirable first novel, despite its depressing subject matter, because of its "detached humour, sensitive awareness, and . . . sheer zest" (*Glasgow Herald*, 17 January 1963, 9).

10. C.B. Cox, editorial, *Critical Quarterly* 8 (Autumn 1966):195.

11. M.L. Rosenthal, "Blood and Plunder," *Spectator*, 30 September 1966, 418.

12. Patricia Meyer Spacks, "A Chronicle of Women," *Hudson Review* 25 (Spring 1972):164.

13. Lucy Rosenthal, "*The Bell Jar*," *Saturday Review*, 24 April 1971, 42.

14. Melvin Maddocks, "A Vacuum Abhorred," *Christian Science Monitor* 15 April 1971, 11; Martha Duffy, "Lady Lazarus," *Time*, 21 June 1971, 87; Tony Tanner, *City of Words* (New York: Harper & Row, 1971), 262.

15. Mason Harris, "*The Bell Jar*," *West Coast Review*, October 1973, 54–56.

16. Helen Dudar, "From Book to Cult," *New York Post*, 2 September 1971, 3, 38.

17. Ronald De Feo, review of *The Bell Jar*, *Modern Occasions* 1 (Fall 1971): 624–25, and Ruth Bauerle, "Plath, at Last," *Plain Dealer*, 25 April 1971, H7.

18. Letter to Ann Davidow, 27 April 1961, from the Smith Library Plath Archive, Smith College, Northampton, Massachusetts.

19. Susan Sniader Lanser, "Beyond *The Bell Jar*: Women Students of the 1970's," *Radical Teacher* 6 (December 1977):41–44; Teresa De Lauretis, "Rebirth in *The Bell Jar*," in *Sylvia Plath: The Critical Heritage*, ed. Linda W. Wagner (London: Routledge & Kegan Paul, 1988), 124–34; Steven Axelrod, *Sylvia Plath: The Wound and the Cure of Words* (Baltimore, Md.: Johns Hopkins University Press, 1990), 231; hereafter cited in text.

20. Lynda K. Bundtzen, *Plath's Incarnations: Woman and the Creative Process* (Ann Arbor: University of Michigan Press, 1983); Susan Bassnett, *Sylvia Plath* (London: Macmillan, 1987); Paula Bennett, "Sylvia Plath: Fusion and the Divided Self," in *My Life a Loaded Gun* (Boston: Beacon Press, 1986), 95–164; Pamela J. Annas, *A Disturbance in Mirrors: The Poetry of Sylvia Plath* (Westport, Conn.: Greenwood Press, 1988).

21. Virginia Woolf, *A Room of One's Own* (New York: Harcourt Brace Jovanovich, 1929), 49–50.

22. *The Bell Jar* (New York: Harper & Row, 1971), 197; hereafter cited in text by page number.

23. Annis Pratt, *Archetypal Patterns in Women's Fiction* (Bloomington:

Indiana University Press, 1981; hereafter cited in text), provides the best discussion of the uses women writers make of conventional structures, genres, and tropes; see also Rachel Blau DuPlessis, *Writing beyond the Ending: Narrative Strategies in Twentieth Century Women's Writing* (Bloomington: Indiana University Press, 1985), and Grace Stewart, *A New Mythos: The Novel of the Artist as Heroine, 1877–1977* (Montreal: Eden Press Women's Publications, 1981).

24. Jerome Hamilton Buckley, *Season of Youth: The Bildungsroman from Dickens to Golding* (Cambridge, Mass.: Harvard University Press, 1974), viii, 18; hereafter cited in text. See C. Hugh Holman, "The *Bildungsroman*, American Style" in *Windows on the World: Essays on American Social Fiction* (Knoxville: University of Tennessee Press, 1979), 168–97, and Henry I. Schvey, "Sylvia Plath's *The Bell Jar: Bildungsroman* or Case History," *Dutch Quarterly Review of Anglo-American Letters* 8 (1978):18–37.

25. Patricia Meyer Spacks, *The Adolescent Idea: Myths of Youth and the Adult Imagination* (New York: Basic Books, 1981), 45; hereafter cited in text.

26. "The Hanging Man," in *The Collected Poems: Sylvia Plath* (New York: Harper & Row, 1981), 141.

27. Letter to her mother, 15 October 1954, in *Letters Home by Sylvia Plath: Correspondence, 1950–1963,* 146.

28. "The Magic Mirror: A Study of the Double in Two of Dostoevsky's Novels," honors thesis, Smith College, 1955. Quoted with permission of the Lilly Library Plath Archive, Indiana University, Bloomington, Indiana. Useful literary commentary on the theme of the double includes Barbara Hill Rigney, *Madness and Sexual Politics in the Feminist Novel* (Madison: University of Wisconsin Press, 1978); Maurice Beebe, *Ivory Towers and Sacred Founts: The Artist as Hero in Fiction from Goethe to Joyce* (New York: New York University Press, 1964); Robert Rogers, *The Double in Literature* (Detroit, Mich.: Wayne State University Press, 1970); Peter M. Axthelm, *The Modern Confessional Novel* (New Haven, Conn.: Yale University Press, 1967); and Irving Massey, *The Gaping Pig: Literature and Metamorphosis* (Berkeley: University of California Press, 1976).

29. Arthur Oberg, *Modern American Lyric—Lowell, Berryman, Creeley, and Plath* (New Brunswick, N.J.: Rutgers University Press, 1978), 177.

30. Anne Cluysenaar, "Post-culture: Pre-culture?" in *British Poetry Since 1960: A Critical Survey,* ed. Michael Schmidt and Grevel Lindop (Oxford, England: Carcanet Press, 1972), 219–21.

31. Letter to Warren Plath, 18 October 1962, in *Letters Home by Sylvia Plath: Correspondence, 1950–1963,* 472.

32. Linda Wagner-Martin, *Sylvia Plath: A Biography* (New York: Simon

& Schuster, 1987), 148.

33. Sandra M. Gilbert, "In Yeats' House: The Death and Resurrection of Sylvia Plath," in *Critical Essays on Sylvia Plath*, ed. Linda W. Wagner (Boston: G. K. Hall, 1984), 204–22; see also Wagner-Martin, *Sylvia Plath: A Biography*, and Steven Axelrod, *Sylvia Plath: The Wound and the Cure of Words*.

34. See also Nancy Chodorow, *The Reproduction of Mothering: Psychoanalysis and the Sociology of Gender* (Berkeley: University of California Press, 1978).

35. Anthony Libby, *Mythologies of Nothing: Mystical Death in American Poetry, 1940–70* (Urbana: University of Illinois Press, 1984), 2–6.

36. "A Comparison," in *Johnny Panic and the Bible of Dreams: Short Stories, Prose, and Diary Excerpts* (New York: Harper & Row, 1977), 61.

37. Ted Hughes, introduction to *Johnny Panic and the Bible of Dreams*, 5.

38. "An Interview: Sylvia Plath Talks with Peter Orr of the British Council," *Plath*, Credo Records, 1975.

39. "The Dark River," manuscript 7R of the Lilly Library Plath Archive, Indiana University.

40. "Sunday at the Mintons'," manuscript 8R of the Lilly Library Plath Archive, Indiana University.

41. "Stone Boy with Dolphin," manuscript 8R of the Lilly Library Plath Archive, Indiana University.

42. "Ocean 1212-W," in *Johnny Panic and the Bible of Dreams*, 23.

43. "Diary Supplement," 13 November 1949, in *Letters Home: Correspondence, 1950–1963*, 40.

44. Melody Zajdel, "Apprenticed in a Bible of Dreams: Sylvia Plath's Short Stories," in *Critical Essays on Sylvia Plath*, 182–93; hereafter cited in text.

45. See Josephine Donovan, "Sexual Politics in Sylvia Plath's Short Stories," *Minnesota Review* (Spring 1973):150–57.

Selected Bibliography

Primary Works

Poetry

The Colossus and Other Poems. New York: Alfred A. Knopf, 1962.
Ariel. New York: Harper & Row, 1966.
Crossing the Water. New York: Harper & Row, 1971.
Winter Trees. New York: Harper & Row, 1972.
The Collected Poems. New York: Harper & Row, 1981.

Prose

The Bell Jar. New York: Harper & Row, 1972. (Originally published only in
    England, 1963, under the pseudonym Victoria Lucas.)
*Johnny Panic and the Bible of Dreams: Short Stories, Prose, and Diary Ex-
    cerpts*. New York: Harper & Row, 1980.

Letters and Journals

Letters Home by Sylvia Plath: Correspondence, 1950–1963, edited with com-
    mentary by Aurelia Schober Plath. New York: Harper & Row, 1975.
The Journals of Sylvia Plath, 1950–1962, ed. Frances McCullough. New
    York: Dial Press, 1982.

Secondary Works

Books Entirely about Sylvia Plath

Aird, Eileen. *Sylvia Plath: Her Life and Work.* New York: Barnes & Noble, 1973. Assessment of Plath's poetry and fiction in relation to her later reputation. Good starting point.

Alexander, Paul. *Rough Magic.* New York: Viking, 1991. Biography that sets up Plath and Hughes as adversaries, and continues past Plath's death in order to probe Hughes's anomie.

Annas, Pamela J. *A Disturbance in Mirrors: The Poetry of Sylvia Plath.* Westport, Conn.: Greenwood Press, 1988. Places Plath's work in a somewhat wider sociological context, viewing the poet's conflicts in relation to her society.

Axelrod, Steven Gould. *Sylvia Plath: The Wound and the Cure of Wounds.* Baltimore, Md.: Johns Hopkins University Press, 1990. Judicious psychoanalytic reading of Plath's major work, with reference to manuscripts, biography, and poet's craft.

Bassnett, Susan. *Sylvia Plath.* London: Macmillan, 1987. Discusses Plath's writing thematically (the importance of family, love, "husband worship," and "the struggle to survive"), considering her representative of her generation.

Bernard, Caroline King. *Sylvia Plath.* Boston: Twayne Publishers, 1978. Chronological reading of Plath's work, with some biography. Focus on poetry.

Broe, Mary Lynn. *Protean Poetic: The Poetry of Sylvia Plath.* Columbia: University of Missouri Press, 1977. Discusses Plath's work by date of writing rather than publication, with close attention to the continuity of her themes.

Bundtzen, Lynda K. *Plath's Incarnations: Woman and the Creative Process.* Ann Arbor: University of Michigan Press, 1983. Critical study that makes use of the manuscript collections at Indiana University and Smith College, incorporating biography where appropriate.

Butscher, Edward. *Sylvia Plath: Method and Madness.* New York: Seabury Press, 1976. Biography that creates polarities between Plath's ambition and her feminine qualities. Unearths some good biographical information.

Holbrook, David. *Sylvia Plath: Poetry and Existence.* London: Athlone, 1976. Emphasizes Plath's psychological processes to the detriment of accurate readings of her work, at times.

Kroll, Judith. *Chapters in a Mythology: The Poetry of Sylvia Plath.* New York: Harper & Row, 1976. One of the few books to have Ted Hughes's direction and aid, Kroll's study provides valuable information about Plath's reading and writing habits and interests.

Selected Bibliography

Rosenblatt, Jon. *Sylvia Plath: The Poetry of Initiation*. Chapel Hill: University of North Carolina Press, 1979. Views Plath's poems as writings and rewritings of the script of death and rebirth (initiation). Comments on the influence of African art and folktale.

Steiner, Nancy Hunter. *A Closer Look at Ariel: A Memory of Sylvia Plath*. New York: Harper's Magazine Press, 1973. Brief memoir about Plath's last years at Smith College, when she and Hunter were close personal friends and roommates. Many of the fictionalized episodes from *The Bell Jar* are recounted in Hunter's book.

Stevenson, Anne. *Bitter Fame: A Life of Sylvia Plath*. Boston: Houghton Mifflin, 1989. A biography that was written with the help of Plath's sister-in-law, Olwyn Hughes, this work presents the poet as seriously ill and mentally unstable most of her life.

Uroff, Margaret Dickie. *Sylvia Plath and Ted Hughes*. Urbana: University of Illinois Press, 1979. Close attention to the reciprocity between the two poets so far as their writing is concerned, with some hypothesis about influences.

Wagner-Martin, Linda. *Sylvia Plath: A Biography*. New York: Simon & Schuster, 1987. Biography that represents Plath as genetically depressive on occasion and otherwise a dynamic writer and student, eager for challenges both aesthetic and personal.

Books Partly about Sylvia Plath

Allen, Mary. *The Necessary Blankness: Women in Major American Fiction of the Sixties*. Urbana: University of Illinois Press, 1976.

Alvarez, A. *The Savage God: A Study of Suicide*. New York: Random House, 1972.

Bennett, Paula. *My Life a Loaded Gun*. Boston: Beacon Press, 1986.

Huf, Linda. *A Portrait of the Artist as a Young Woman: The Writer as Heroine in American Literature*. New York: Ungar, 1983.

Juhasz, Suzanne. *Naked and Fiery Forms, Modern American Poetry by Women: A New Tradition*. New York: Harper Colophon, 1976.

Karl, Frederick R. *American Fictions, 1940–1980: A Comprehensive History and Critical Evaluation*. New York: Harper & Row, 1983.

Markey, Janice. *A New Tradition? The Poetry of Sylvia Plath, Anne Sexton, and Adrienne Rich*. New York: Peter Lang, 1985.

Miller, Alice. *For Your Own Good: Hidden Cruelty in Childrearing and the Roots of Violence*. New York: Farrar, Straus & Giroux, 1983.

Moers, Ellen. *Literary Women*. Garden City, N.Y.: Doubleday, 1976.

Oberg, Arthur. *Modern American Lyric: Lowell, Berryman, Creeley, and Plath*. New Brunswick, N.J.: Rutgers University Press, 1978.

Pratt, Annis. *Archetypal Patterns in Women's Fiction*. Bloomington: Indiana University Press, 1981.

Simpson, Louis. *A Revolution in Taste*. New York: Macmillan, 1978.

Stewart, Grace. *A New Mythos: The Novel of the Artist as Heroine, 1877–1977*. Montreal: Eden Press Women's Publications, 1981.

Tanner, Tony. *City of Words*. New York: Harper & Row, 1971.

Werner, Craig. *Paradoxical Resolutions: American Fiction since James Joyce*. Urbana: University of Illinois Press, 1982.

Yalom, Marilyn. *Maternity, Mortality, and the Literature of Madness*. University Park: Pennsylvania State University Press, 1985.

Essay Collections of Criticism on Plath

Alexander, Paul, ed. *Ariel Ascending: Writings about Sylvia Plath*. New York: Harper & Row, 1984.

Bloom, Harold, ed. *Sylvia Plath*. New York: Chelsea House, 1989.

Butscher, Edward, ed. *Sylvia Plath: The Woman and the Work*. New York: Dodd, Mead, 1977.

Lane, Gary, ed. *Sylvia Plath: New Views on the Poetry*. Baltimore, Md.: Johns Hopkins University Press, 1979.

Newman, Charles, ed. *The Art of Sylvia Plath: A Symposium*. Reprinted from *Tri-Quarterly*. Bloomington: Indiana University Press, 1970.

Wagner, Linda W., ed. *Critical Essays on Sylvia Plath*. Boston: G. K. Hall, 1984.

Wagner-Martin, Linda, ed. *Sylvia Plath: The Critical Heritage*. London: Routledge & Kegan Paul, 1988.

Essays

Ames, Lois. "Notes toward a Biography." In *The Art of Sylvia Plath: A Symposium*, edited by Charles Newman (reprinted from *Tri-Quarterly*), 155–73. Bloomington: Indiana University Press, 1970.

———. "Sylvia Plath: A Biographical Note." In *The Bell Jar*, 203–16. New York: Harper & Row, 1971.

Atwood, Margaret. "Poet's Prose." *New York Times Book Review*, 28 January 1979, 10, 31.

Broe, Mary Lynn. "A Subtle Psychic Bond: The Mother Figure in Sylvia Plath's

Selected Bibliography

Poetry." In *The Lost Tradition: Mothers and Daughters in Literature*, ed. Cathy N. Davidson and E. M. Broner, 217–30. New York: Ungar, 1980.

Burgess, Anthony. "Transatlantic Englishmen." *Observer*, January 1963, 22.

Burton, Deirdre. "Through Glass Darkly, through Dark Glasses: On Stylistics and Political Commitment—via a Study of a Passage from Sylvia Plath's *The Bell Jar*." In *Language and Literature: An Introductory Reader in Stylistics*, ed. Ronald Carter, 195–214. London: Allen & Unwin, 1982.

Butler, Rupert. "New American Fiction: Three Disappointing Novels—but One Good One." *Time and Tide*, 31 January 1963, 34.

De Lauretis, Teresa. "Rebirth in *The Bell Jar*." *Women's Studies* 3 (1975): 173–83.

Donovan, Josephine. "Sexual Politics in Sylvia Plath's Short Stories." *Minnesota Review* 4 (Spring 1973): 150–57.

Dudar, Helen. "From Book to Cult." *New York Post*, 2 September 1971, 3, 38.

Duffy, Martha. "Lady Lazarus." *Time*, 27 June 1971, 87.

Gilbert, Sandra M. "A Fine, White Flying Myth: The Life/Work of Sylvia Plath." In *Shakespeare's Sisters: Feminist Essays on Women Poets*, ed. Sandra M. Gilbert and Susan Gubar, 245–60. Bloomington: Indiana University Press, 1979.

Harris, Mason. *"The Bell Jar."* *West Coast Review*, October 1973, 54–56.

Higgins, Judith. "Sylvia Plath's Growing Popularity with College Students." *University: A Princeton Quarterly* 58 (Fall 1973):28–33, 48.

Horovitz, Israel. "Some God Got Hold of Me." *Village Voice*, 28 October 1971, 27–30.

———. "Success in Spite of Suicide." *Village Voice*, 4 November 1971, 21–22, 38.

Hughes, Ted. Foreword to *The Journals of Sylvia Plath, 1950–62*, ed. Frances McCullough. New York: Dial Press, 1982.

———. Introduction to *The Collected Poems of Sylvia Plath*, ed. Ted Hughes. New York: Harper & Row, 1981.

———. Introduction to *Johnny Panic and the Bible of Dreams: Short Stories, Prose, and Diary Excerpts*. New York: Harper & Row, 1979.

———. "Note" (introducing 10 poems by Plath). *Encounter* 21 (October 1963):45.

———. "Notes on the Chronological Order of Sylvia Plath's Poems." In Newman, 187–95.

———. "Sylvia Plath." *Poetry Book Society Bulletin* 44 (February 1965).

———. "Sylvia Plath and Her Journals." In *Ariel Ascending: Writings about*

Sylvia Plath, edited by Paul Alexander. 152–64. New York: Harper & Row, 1984.

———. "Sylvia Plath's *Crossing the Water*: Some Reflections." *Critical Quarterly*, 13 (Summer 1971): 165–72.

———. "Winter Trees." Poetry Book Society Bulletin 70 (Autumn 1971).

Klein, Elinor. "A Friend Recalls Sylvia Plath." *Glamour*, November 1966, 168–84.

Lerner, Laurence. "New Novels." *Listener*, 31 January 1963, 215.

Maddocks, Melvin. "A Vacuum Abhorred." *Christian Science Monitor*, 15 April 1971, 11.

Mademoiselle. College Board issue, August 1953.

Martin, Elaine. "Mothers, Madness, and the Middle Class in *The Bell Jar* and *Les Mots pour le Dire*." *French-American Review* 5 (Spring 1981):24–47.

Martin, Wendy. " 'God's Lioness': Sylvia Plath, Her Prose and Poetry." *Women's Studies* 1 (1973):191–98.

Perloff, Marjorie. "Icon of the Fifties." *Parnassus* 12 and 13 (1985):282–85.

Rosenstein, Harriet. "Reconsidering Sylvia Plath." *Ms.*, September 1972, 45–51, 96–99.

Rosenthal, Lucy. "The Bell Jar," Saturday Review, 24 April 1971, 42.

Rosenthal, M. L. "Blood and Plunder." *Spectator*, 30 September 1966, 418.

———, and Sally M. Gall. " 'Pure? What Does It Mean?' Notes on Sylvia Plath's Poetic Art." *American Poetry Review* 7 (1978):37–40.

Schvey, Henry I. "Sylvia Plath's *The Bell Jar: Bildungsroman* or Case History." *Dutch Quarterly Review of Anglo-American Letters* 8 (1978):18–37.

Shook, Margaret. "Sylvia Plath: The Poet and the College." *Smith Alumnae Quarterly* 63 (April 1972):4–9.

Smith, Stan. "Attitudes Counterfeiting Life: The Irony of Artifice in Sylvia Plath's *The Bell Jar*." *Critical Quarterly* 17 (Autumn 1975):247–60.

Staton, Shirley F. "The Great Divide: Gender in Sylvia Plath's Short Fiction." *Women and Literature* 2 (1982):206–221.

Taubman, Robert. "Anti-heroes." *New Statesman*, 25 January 1963, 127–28.

Van Dyne, Susan R. "Fueling the Phoenix Fire: The Manuscripts of Sylvia Plath's 'Lady Lazarus.' " *Massachusetts Review* 27 (Winter 1983):395–410.

———. "Rekindling the Past in Sylvia Plath's 'Burning the Letters.' " *Centennial Review* 32 (Summer 1988):250–65.

Wagner, Linda W. "45 Mercy Street and Other Vacant Houses." In *American Literature: The New England Heritage*, ed. James Nagel and Richard Astro, 145–65. New York: Garland, 1981.

———. "Modern American Literature: The Poetics of the Individual Voice."

Centennial Review 21 (Fall 1977):333–54.

———. "Plath's *The Bell Jar* as Female *Bildungsroman.*" *Women's Studies* 12 (February 1986):55–68.

———. "Plath's *Ladies' Home Journal* Syndrome." *Journal of American Culture* 7 (Spring–Summer 1984):32–38.

———. "Sylvia Plath's Specialness in Her Short Stories." *Journal of Narrative Technique* 15 (Winter 1985):1–14.

Whittier, Gayle. "The Divided Woman and Generic Doubleness in *The Bell Jar.*" *Women's Studies* 3 (1976):127–46.

Zajdel, Melody. "Apprenticed in a Bible of Dreams: Sylvia Plath's Short Stories." In *Critical Essays on Sylvia Plath*, 182–93.

Bibliography

Lane, Gary, and Maria Stevens. *Sylvia Plath: A Bibliography.* Metuchen, N.J.: Scarecrow Press, 1978.

Matovich, Richard M., ed. *A Concordance to the Collected Poems of Sylvia Plath.* New York: Garland Press, 1986.

Meyering, Sheryl. *Sylvia Plath: A Reference Guide, 1973–1988.* Boston: G. K. Hall, 1990.

Tabor, Stephen. *Sylvia Plath: An Analytical Bibliography.* London: Mansell, 1987.

Walsh, Thomas P., and Cameron Northouse. *Sylvia Plath and Anne Sexton: A Reference Guide.* Boston: G. K. Hall, 1974.

Index

Index

THE AUTHOR

Linda Wagner-Martin is Hanes Professor of English and Comparative Literature at the University of North Carolina, Chapel Hill. She has recently been working at the Rockefeller Bellagio Center in Italy on her revisionist biography of Gertrude Stein and her family, under the auspices of the American Philosophical Society and the National Endowment for the Humanities. Recent books include her biography of Sylvia Plath (1987), her survey *The Modern American Novel, 1914–1945* (Twayne, 1989), and collections on the writing of both Anne Sexton and Denise Levertov. An earlier volume in this series was *The House of Mirth: A Novel of Admonition*. Wagner-Martin has been a Guggenheim fellow and a Bunting Institute fellow, and taught previously at Michigan State University, Bowling Green State University, and Wayne State University.